WHAT'S SO GREAT ABOUT AMERICA

DINESH D'SOUZA

WHAT'S SO GREAT ABOUT AMERICA

Since 1947
**REGNERY
PUBLISHING, INC.**
An Eagle Publishing Company • Washington, DC

Library of Congress Cataloging-in-Publication Data

D'Souza, Dinesh.
What's so great about America / Dinesh D'Souza
p. cm.
Includes index.
ISBN 0-89526-153-7
1. United States—Civilization. 2. National characteristics,
American. 3. Civilization, Western. I. Title.
E169.1 .D78 2001
973—dc21
2002000672

Published in the United States by
Regnery Publishing, Inc.
An Eagle Publishing Company
One Massachusetts Avenue, NW
Washington, DC 20001

Visit us at www.regnery.com

Distributed to the trade by
National Book Network
4720-A Boston Way
Lanham, MD 20706

Printed on acid-free paper
Manufactured in the United States of America

10 9 8 7 6 5 4 3 2 1

Books are available in quantity for promotional or premium use.
Write to Director of Special Sales, Regnery Publishing, Inc.,
One Massachusetts Avenue, NW, Washington, DC 20001,
for information on discounts and terms or call (202) 216-0600

For Danielle
Who Will One Day Understand

CONTENTS

A FUNERAL ORATION
Pericles' Dilemma, and Ours

In 430 B.C., shortly after the outbreak of the Peloponnesian War, Pericles delivered a funeral oration to the people of Athens.[1] His dilemma was the classic one faced by free peoples throughout history: how to articulate the blessings of freedom which are usually taken for granted, how to communicate to citizens the necessity of making sacrifices—including the ultimate sacrifice of one's life—in the name of freedom, and how a society accustomed to the pleasures of private life can prevail against a more militaristic regime inured to hardship whose fighters are cheerfully willing to endure death.

Sound familiar? This is what Pericles said: "Our system of government does not copy the institutions of its neighbors. It is more the case of our being a model to others, than of our imitating anyone." Athens, in other words, has a unique civilization that holds itself up as a universal model for civilized peoples everywhere.

What are the ingredients of that civilization? "When it is a question of settling disputes, everyone is equal before the law. When it is a question of putting one person before another in positions of public responsibility, what counts is not membership in a particular class, but the actual ability which the man possesses." Equality and meritocracy are, in Pericles' view, two of the defining characteristics of ancient Athens.

Moreover, "just as our political life is free and open, so is our day-to-day life in our relations with each other. We do not get into a state with our next-door neighbor if he enjoys himself in his own way. We are free and tolerant in our private lives, but in public affairs we keep to the law. That is because it commands our deep respect." Athens is a freedom-loving society, but its liberty is within the bounds of the law. Free people choose to obey the law because they see it as legitimate and for their benefit, rather than arbitrary.

Athens is also a commercial civilization that trades freely with its neighbors. "The greatness of our city brings it about that all the good things from all over the world flow in to us, so that it seems just as natural to enjoy foreign goods as our own local products." There is an easy traffic of peoples across state boundaries. "Our city is open to the world, and we have no periodical deportations in order to prevent people observing or finding out secrets which might be of military advantage to the enemy."

This liberality of mind and policy, Pericles concedes, makes Athens vulnerable to enemies who seem leaner, hungrier, and hardier. "The Spartans, from their earliest boyhood, are submitted to the most laborious training in courage." Even so, Pericles emphasizes that the Athenians "pass our lives without all these restrictions, and yet are just as ready to face the same dangers as they are."

The reason is that "others are brave out of ignorance, but the man who can most truly be accounted brave is he who best knows the meaning of what is sweet in life and of what is terrible, and then goes out undeterred to meet what is to come." Pericles calls upon the Athenians to recognize that theirs is the city that makes the quest for wisdom and the good life possible, for themselves and for their children, and he calls upon citizens to develop an *eros* for their city, a deep and abiding love that will justify and make possible the sacrifices that must be made to preserve Athenian liberty and the Athenian way of life.

"What I would ask is that you should fix your eyes every day on the greatness of Athens as she really is, and should fall in love with her." The greatness of Athens *as she really is*. Even as he presents a somewhat idealized view of Athens, Pericles is saying that ultimately we fight for our country not in the name of some abstract theory, not even in the name of founding myths and constitutions, but in the name of the kind of society that we live in, and the kind of life that it makes possible for us.

America today is in the position of the ancient Athenians, facing in the militants of the Islamic world a new kind of Sparta. What is needed, therefore, is an examination of the source of the conflict, of the nature of the enemy. But what is needed, most of all, is an understanding of the moral basis of Western civilization, of what makes the American experiment historically unique, and of what makes American life *as it is lived today* the best life that our world has to offer. Only then can we know what is at stake in this war and what we possess that is worth fighting for.

WHAT'S SO GREAT
ABOUT AMERICA

CHAPTER ONE

WHY THEY HATE US
America and Its Enemies

The cry that comes from the heart of the believer
overcomes everything, even the White House.

—AYATOLLAH KHOMEINI

BEFORE THE TERRORISTS DESTROYED THE WORLD TRADE
Center, crashed a plane into the Pentagon, and began their
campaign to bring to America the horrors of the war-
ravaged Middle East, life in the United States was placid and even
a little boring. The dominant issue in politics was the Social Security lockbox, an especially curious subject of dispute since no such
lockbox exists or has ever existed. For diversion and entertainment, Americans could follow the Gary Condit sex scandal or
watch "reality TV" shows like *Survivor*. Newspapers devoted
front-page reports to such issues as road rage, a man bitten by a
shark, and the revelation that overage kids were playing Little
League baseball. The biggest issue in the airline industry involved
something called "economy class syndrome." Essentially this

referred to rather obese people sitting in coach class and fretting that during long flights their legs became stiff.

All this triviality and absurdity was swept aside by the hijackers. In an act of supreme chutzpah, coordination, and technical skill, nineteen men seized control of four commercial jet planes, crashed two into the Twin Towers of the World Trade Center, and rammed one into the shoulder of the Pentagon. The fourth plane did not find its target—possibly the White House or Camp David—but crashed into the woods of Pennsylvania. In a single day of infamy—September 11, 2001—the terrorists had killed more than three thousand people.

Not since Pearl Harbor, which provoked American entry into World War II, had America been directly attacked in this way by a foreign power. But even that was different. Pearl Harbor is in Hawaii, not on the American mainland. Moreover, the attack on Pearl Harbor was a military operation directed against the U.S. Navy. By contrast, the terrorists struck New York City, and most of the people they killed were civilians. One would have to go back more than a century, to the Civil War, to count such large numbers of American casualties on a single day. As for civilian casualties, the citizens of the United States had never endured such mayhem. Historian David McCullough called September 11, 2001, the worst day in America's history.

Now, amidst our grief and sad memories, we find ourselves at war against the forces of terrorism. It is an overt war, such as we saw in the overthrow of the Taliban regime, as well as a covert war, with secret campaigns to identify and destroy enemy networks and cells. It is a war that has come home to America, as people cope with fears of further attacks, including those involving biological, chemical, and—God forbid—nuclear weapons. Moreover, this is a new kind of war against an enemy that refuses to identify himself. Our enemy is a terrorist regime that inhabits many countries, including the United States. It is made up of very strange people most of whose names we do not yet know and whose motives and inspiration remain unclear to us. And the enemy conducts its operations in the name of Islam, one of the world's great religions and a very old civilization that has some-how now become an incubator of fanaticism and terrorism.

Know your enemy, Clausewitz instructs us, and then you will be able to fight him. Despite our early success in Afghan-istan, it is not clear that we understand our enemy very well. Indeed, America's incomprehension of the enemy became appar-ent in the days immediately following September 11, with the insis-tence of our leaders and pundits that the terrorists were "cowards" or "faceless cowards." President Bush first used this term, which was then repeated by many others. The reasoning is that the ter-rorists cravenly targeted women and children. But of course the terrorists did no such thing. They didn't really care who was on the hijacked planes or in the World Trade Center. As it hap-pened, most of their victims were men. Their targets were the symbols of American capitalism and of the American govern-ment. One of them was the Pentagon, by any reckoning a mili-tary target. Usually we consider people who pick on women and children cowardly because they are trying to avoid harm to them-selves. But in this case the terrorists went to their deaths with certainty and apparent equanimity. Like the Japanese kamikazes, the terrorists were certainly fanatical, but cowards they were not.

A second enduring myth about the terrorists is that they were poor, miserable souls who performed these terrible actions because they were desperate or more likely insane. Several commentators argued that the terrorists are drawn from "the wretched of the earth." In this view, they strike out against the affluent West because they have nothing to live for. Television host Bill O'Reilly carried this logic even further. He could not consider the terrorists brave, O'Reilly said, because they labored under the illusion that they were going straight to heaven, where they would be attended by countless nubile virgins. This, in O'Reilly's view, was simply "nuts."

But these theories do not square with the facts. Indeed, it is irrational and reckless to dismiss the terrorists in this way. O'Reilly's lunacy theory can be tested by releasing a bunch of mentally handicapped people from one of our asylums. Could they have pulled off what the terrorists did? Of course not. The unnerving reality is that the terrorists were educated people who knew how to fly planes. They had lived in the West and been exposed to the West. Some of them, like Muhammad Atta, were raised in secular households. Many came from well-off families. Indeed, the ringleader, Osama bin Laden, had a reported net worth of more than $100 million. Normally men with bin Laden's bank account can be found in Monaco or St. Tropez, sailing yachts with beautiful women on each arm. Bin Laden, by contrast, spent the past several years living in a cave in Afghanistan.

What motivates such men? One vital clue is the diary composed by Muhammad Atta and circulated to the other terrorists prior to the attack. The FBI found it in Atta's apartment. Out of respect for Allah, it says, clean your body, shave off excess hair, wear cologne, and "tighten your shoes." Read the Koran and "pray through the night" in order to "purify your soul from all unclean things." Try and detach yourself from this world because "the time for play is over." Keep a steadfast mind because "anything that happens to you could never be avoided, and what did not happen to you could never have happened to you." On the morning of the attack, "pray the morning prayer" and "do not leave your apartment unless you have performed ablution." Pray as you enter the plane and recite verses from the Koran. Ask God to forgive your sins and to give you the victory. Clench your teeth as you prepare for the attack. Shout "Allahu Akbar." Strike your enemy above the neck, as the Koran instructs. Moreover, "if you slaughter, do not cause the discomfort of those you are killing, because this is one of the practices of the prophet, peace be upon him." Finally, "You should feel complete tranquility, because the time between you and your marriage in heaven is very short."[1]

These are not the instructions of cowards or lunatics, but of deeply religious Muslims. They were armed with an idea, and their colleagues have the weapons, the strategy, and the ruthlessness that are required to take on the United States and the West. It is a mistake to regard them as "suicides" in the traditional sense. A suicidal person is one who does not want to live. These men wanted to live, but they were prepared to give their life for something they deemed higher. This in itself is not contemptible or ridiculous; indeed, it raises the question of what we in America would be willing to give our lives for. No serious patriotism is possible that does not attempt to answer that question.

It is difficult for those of us who live in a largely secular society to understand that people would willingly—even happily—give their lives for their faith. When a few people show such tendencies, we deem them extremists; when large numbers of people do, we convince ourselves that they have been brainwashed. They say they are acting in the name of Allah, but we insist that this is not their real motive; they are being manipulated by elites. They believe they are martyrs, but we pronounce that they are not really Muslims. President Bush even suggested that they were betraying their faith. British prime minister Tony Blair has said he regrets the term "Islamic terrorists" because the vast majority of Muslims are not terrorists.[2]

True Islam, many pundits noted, is a religion of peace. As Nada El Sawy, an Arab-American, wrote in *Newsweek*, "Muslims who kill in the name of their beliefs are not true Muslims."[3] Advocates of this position point out that the term *jihad* does not mean "holy war": it refers to a moral struggle to conquer the evil in oneself. So if Islam wasn't the driving force behind the attacks, what was? The *New Yorker* comfortingly concluded, "This is a conflict that pits all of civilized society against a comparatively small, essentially stateless band of murderous outlaws."[4]

These statements may have been made for the political purpose of isolating the terrorists and keeping together an alliance against terrorism that includes several Muslim countries. But they are profoundly misleading. Political unity is important, but so is mental clarity and honesty. If we misunderstand what is driving our enemy, then our strategy in fighting him is likely to be inadequate. Despite the early success of the U.S. military campaign, it is not clear that America has a well-conceived long-term strategy for getting rid of terrorism. Moreover, honesty, together with an informed sense of history, obliges us to admit that the things that we have been saying about Islam are half-truths, and dangerous half-truths at that.

Tony Blair is right that the vast majority of Muslims are not terrorists, but it is equally a fact that the vast majority of terrorists are Muslims. Indeed, most of the states that the U.S. government classifies as "terrorist" or "rogue" states, such as Iraq, Iran, Syria, Libya, and the Sudan, fall within the Muslim world. While Americans insist that the terrorists are fringe figures— similar perhaps to our Ku Klux Klan—the evidence is that they enjoy considerable support in their part of the globe. Immediately following the attack, bin Laden became a folk hero in the Islamic world. The actions of the terrorists were cheered in Iraq, Libya, and among many supporters of the Palestine Liberation Organization. In Gaza, for example, a poll showed that 78 percent of Palestinians supported the attacks.[5] Another poll showed that 83 percent of Pakistanis sympathize with bin Laden's al Qaeda group and oppose the United States' military response.[6] Even the governments of Muslim countries that are allied with the U.S. in the war against terrorism have proved very reluctant to involve themselves in the fighting. Nor have the leading authorities of any Muslim country condemned the terrorists as acting in violation of the principles of Islam.

The reason for such waffling is that our allies know that terrorism and anti-Americanism have substantial support among the population in the Islamic world, even in so-called moderate Arab countries. Virtually the entire Muslim world has, over the past few decades, experienced a religious resurgence—what we may term the revival of Islamic fundamentalism.[7] The authority of the fundamentalists is not confined to a few countries, such as Iran and the Sudan. Of the twenty-two nations of the Muslim world, none is exempt from fundamentalist influence. This movement is powerful enough, in numbers and in political intensity, to threaten the stability of countries allied with the United States, like Pakistan, Egypt, and Saudi Arabia. Indeed, the leadership of those countries is constantly on the defensive against the militants; it is they—not the terrorists or the militants—who are under suspicion for betraying Islam.

The terrorists and their supporters don't have to prove their bona fides. They do what they do in the name of *jihad*, a term that literally means "striving." Some Muslims, especially in the modern era, understand *jihad* as a form of internal warfare in the soul against sin. But the Koran itself urges Muslims to "slay the idolaters wherever you find them. Seize them, besiege them, and lie in ambush everywhere for them."[8] In his classic work, *The Muqaddimah*, the influential Muslim writer Ibn Khaldun asserts, "In the Muslim community, holy war is a religious duty, because of the obligation to convert everybody to Islam either by persuasion or by force."[9] These passages convey how Muslims themselves have usually understood their religious mission. Historian Bernard Lewis writes that the traditional Islamic view, upheld by the vast majority of jurists and commentators, is that *jihad* usually refers to an armed struggle against infidels and apostates. Lewis writes:

> In the Muslim worldview the basic division of mankind is into the House of Islam (Dar al-Islam) and the House of

War (Dar al-Harb). Ideally the House of Islam is conceived as a single community. The logic of Islamic law, however, does not recognize the permanent existence of any other polity outside Islam. In time, in the Muslim view, all mankind will accept Islam or submit to Islamic rule. A treaty of peace between the Muslim state and a non-Muslim state was thus in theory impossible. Such a truce, according to the jurists, could only be provisional. The name given by the Muslim jurists to this struggle is *jihad*.[10]

The clear implication of Lewis's remarks is that the terrorists who profess the name of Allah and proclaim *jihad* are operating squarely within the Islamic tradition. Indeed, they are performing what Islam has typically held to be a religious duty. Of course it could be pointed out that there are millions of Muslims who do not agree with this view of Islam. They prefer what may be termed the "*jihad* of the heart" or perhaps the "*jihad* of the pen" to the "*jihad* of the sword." But traditionally Islam has embraced all these forms of *jihad* as legitimate, so that the only reasonable conclusion is that many Muslims today, both in the West and in the Islamic world, no longer profess Islam in its traditional sense.[11] In a word, they are liberals, not in the Michael Dukakis connotation, but in the classic meaning of the term. From the point of view of the bin Ladens of the world, these people are apostates for diluting the faith and refusing to do battle against the infidels.

I realize that terms like "apostate" and "infidel" sound harshly unfamiliar to the Western ear. There is something strange and antique about them, as if they belong to the world of our ancestors. And of course they do. A thousand years ago, during the time of the Crusades, the ancestors of the West understood their Islamic foe very well. Nobody spoke of "the West" at that time; they spoke of "Christendom." It was a time, one may say, when the Christians, too, had their *jihad*, and it was aimed at the reconquest of the Holy Land. For Christians, the crusades combined two traditional practices, pilgrimage and holy war. Kings and popes alike proclaimed that those who died in battle were martyrs for the faith and would go straight to heaven.

There are important differences, of course, between Islam and Christianity, and the religious armies who faced each other in the eleventh and twelfth centuries were very conscious of them. But they were also conscious of the deep similarities between the two faiths. Islam and Christianity are both monotheistic, and they are the only two religions that can truly be called universal. Judaism is a religion for God's chosen people, and God's instructions are intended for them, not for anyone else. Hinduism is largely confined to India and the surrounding areas. Buddhism has longer tentacles, but it too is largely an Asian religion with a few adherents in the West. Confucianism is not really a religion, and in any case it has a limited reach. Christianity and Islam, by contrast, believe in a universal truth handed down by God that is true for all people in all places at all times. Believing themselves in possession of this exclusive truth, Christians and Muslims have historically sought to inform the whole world of their truth and to bring them to the one true faith. During the Crusades they both had a name for each other, "infidel." It was the same name, and both sides interpreted it the same way. Islam and Christianity clashed not because they failed to understand each other but because they understood each other perfectly well.

But a lot has happened since the twelfth century, and we have forgotten a lot of things. American culture is rather present oriented, and even what happened in the 1980s now seems dated. It is time that we started to learn and to remember because our enemies do. When bin Laden invokes the name of Salah-al-Din (Saladin), he is drawing inspiration from the great twelfth-century Muslim general who threw back the Crusaders and recaptured Jerusalem. In his videotaped statement released on Al Jazeera television, bin Laden said Americans should get used to suffering because "our Islamic nation has been tasting the same for more than 80 years." He was referring to the dismembering of the Ottoman Empire, the last of the great Muslim empires, by the victorious European forces after World War I.

Say what you will about the terrorists, they know who they are and where they are coming from. And behind their physical attack on America and the West is an intellectual attack, one that we should understand and be prepared to answer.

One reason the terrorist assault startled Americans so much is that it occurred at a time when American ideas and American influence seemed to be spreading irresistibly throughout the world. The zeitgeist was captured by Francis Fukuyama in his bestselling book *The End of History and the Last Man*. Fukuyama argued that the world was moving decisively in the direction of liberal, capitalist democracy.[12] In Fukuyama's view, history had ended not in the sense that important things would cease to happen, but in the sense that the grand ideological conflicts of the past had been forever settled. Of course the pace of liberalization would vary, but the outcome was inevitable. The destiny of Homo sapiens had been resolved. We were headed for what may be termed Planet America.

Fukuyama's thesis, advanced in the early 1990s, seemed consistent with the remarkable events going on in the world. The collapse of the Soviet Union left America as the world's sole superpower, with unrivaled military superiority. The discrediting of socialism meant that there was no conceivable alternative to capitalism, and all the countries of the world seemed destined to be integrated into a single global economy. Dictatorships crumbled in many parts the world, especially in Eastern Europe and Latin America, and were replaced by democratic regimes. America launched the silicon revolution and continues to dominate the world in technology. And American ideas and American culture have captured the imagination of young people around the world and made deep inroads into previously remote outposts in Asia, Africa, Latin America, and the Middle East.

These are undeniable and hugely important facts, but the complacent confidence of the Planet America thesis has been shaken. The Cold War is over, and yet the world has become a more dangerous place. Americans, never particularly attentive to the rest of the world, have become acutely aware that there are powerful currents of resistance to globalization and Americanization. There are lots of people who do not want to become like us, and many people, especially in the Muslim world, apparently hate our guts and want to wipe us off the face of the earth. This realization, for Americans, comes as a surprise.

In his 1997 book *The Clash of Civilizations and the Remaking of World Order*, Samuel Huntington warned that America and the West should not arrogantly assume that the rest of the world would uncritically embrace the principles of Judeo-Christian civilization. Huntington disputed the thesis of "the end of history" and pointed out that the great victories won in recent years by liberalism and democracy were mainly in Latin America and Eastern Europe, regions of the world that were within the traditional orbit of the Judeo-Christian West. Huntington argued that in the post–Cold War world, the most dangerous conflicts would occur "across the fault lines between the world's major civilizations."[13] Huntington identified civilizations mainly in terms of religion: Hindu civilization, Confucian civilization, Islamic civilization. Given the deep differences among these religious tribes, Huntington predicted that they were bound to quarrel.

So who is right, Fukuyama or Huntington? This is one of the questions that this book will try to answer. But first let us examine the three main currents of foreign opposition to the spread of American influence.

First, the European school. Actually this may be more precisely described as the French school, although it has sympathizers in other European countries. The French seem to be outraged by the idea that any single nation, let alone the United States, should enjoy global domination. The French foreign minister, Hubert Vedrine, termed the United States a "hyperpower" and scorned its "arrogance." The French are not against arrogance per se, but in the case of the United States they regard the arrogance as completely unjustified. For the French, the grotesque symbol of Americanization is McDonald's, and many French citizens cheered in 1999 when a sheep farmer named José Bové trashed a McDonald's in France. The French worry that the spread of English threatens the future of the French language and, even more precious, French culture. Their anti-Americanization is based on a strong belief in French cultural superiority combined with a fear that their great culture is being dissolved in the global marketplace.

Most Americans find it hard to take the French critique seriously, coming as it does from men who carry handbags. French anti-Americanism is also a political device to legitimate the use of tariffs, thus protecting French products that cannot compete in the global marketplace. But at the same time the French have a point when they object to the obliteration of local cultures and the homogenization of the planet in the name of globalization and Americanization. Probably we can also agree that the world would be a worse place without the French language and French cuisine, although whether we could do without French films and French intellectuals is open to dispute.

A second and more troubling critique of America comes from what may be termed the Asian school. This view, which has advocates in Singapore and Malaysia and, most important, China, holds that America and the West have solved the economic problem but they have not solved the cultural problem. As Lee Kuan Yew, the former prime minister of Singapore, has argued, America has generated a lot of material prosperity, but that has been accompanied by social and moral decline. Champions of the Asian school hold that they have figured out a way to combine material well-being with social order. In Singapore, for example, you are encouraged to engage in commerce, but there is no chewing gum in public and if you paint graffiti on cars, as one American visitor did, you will be publicly caned. The result, advocates of the Asian school say, is that people can enjoy a high standard of living but without the crime, illegitimacy, and vulgarity that are believed to debase life in the West.

The "Asian values" paradigm is often viewed as an excuse for dictatorship. Admittedly it serves the interest of Asian despots to portray democracy as a debauched system of government, so that they can justify keeping political power in their own hands. But it is hard to deny that there are powerful elements of truth in the way that Lee Kuan Yew and others portray America and the West. That there may be an alternative model better suited to the human desire for prosperity, safety, and public decency cannot be rejected out of hand. Lee Kuan Yew's slogan for this is "modernization without Westernization."[14]

Undoubtedly the most comprehensive and ferocious attack on America comes from what may be termed the Islamic school. From what Americans hear of this group, with its slogans that we are the Great Satan, land of the infidels, and so on, it does not seem that this is a very sophisticated critique of Western society. On television we see protesters in Iraq, Iran, and Pakistan, and they seem like a bunch of jobless fanatics. But behind these demonstrators who chant and burn American flags in the street, there is a considered argument against America that should not be lightly dismissed. Americans should not assume that because they haven't heard much of this argument, it does not exist or has no intellectual merit.

On the surface it seems that the Islamic critique is mainly focused on American foreign policy. Certainly many Muslims angrily object to the degree of U.S. political and financial support for Israel. "We consider America and Israel to be one country," one Palestinian man told CNN. "When the Israelis burn our homes and kill our children, we know that it is your weapons, your money and your helicopters that are making this happen." Interestingly the Palestinian problem was not initially a big concern for bin Laden; he seemed more exercised about the effect of American sanctions on the Iraqi people and about the presence of American troops in Saudi Arabia, the "holy soil of Islam." Another issue for bin Laden, which resonates especially with Muslim intellectuals, is the proclaimed hypocrisy of America. In this view, the United States piously invokes principles of democracy and human rights while supporting undemocratic regimes, such as those of Pakistan, Egypt, and Saudi Arabia, that do not hesitate to trample on human rights. Probably bin Laden strikes the biggest chord with the man in the Arab street when he blames the poverty and degradation of the Islamic world on Western and specifically American oppression.

Clearly the foreign policy element is important, but there is much more to the Islamic critique than that. Once we begin to peruse the newspapers and listen to the public discussion in the Muslim world, and once we read the thinkers who are shaping the mind of Islamic fundamentalism, we realize that here is an intelligent and even profound assault on the very basis of America and the West. Indeed, the Islamic critique, at its best, shows a deep understanding of America's fundamental principles—which is more than one can say about the American understanding of Islamic principles. This critique deserves careful attention not only because of its intrinsic power but also because it is the guiding force behind the *jihad* factories—the countless mosques and religious schools throughout the Muslim world that are teaching such violent hatred of America.

Islamic critics recognize that other people around the world are trying selectively to import aspects of America and the West while rejecting other aspects that they do not like. Thus the Chinese, the Indians, the Africans, and the Latin Americans all want some of what the West has to offer—especially technology and prosperity—but they want to keep out other things. "Modernization without Westernization" expresses a widespread desire to preserve the treasured elements of one's own culture and identity in the face of Westernization.

But the Islamic thinkers argue that selective Westernization is an illusion. In their view modernity *is* Western, and they regard as naïve the notion that one can import what one likes from America while keeping out what one dislikes. The Islamic argument is that the West is based on principles that are radically different from those of traditional societies. In this view, America is a subversive idea that, if admitted into a society, will produce tremendous and uncontrollable social upheaval. It will eliminate the religious basis for society, it will undermine traditional hierarchies, it will displace cherished values, and it will produce a society unrecognizable from the one it destroyed. As bin Laden himself put it, Islam is facing the greatest threat to its survival since the days of the prophet Muhammad.

He's right. And the Islamic thinkers who fear the dissolution of their traditional societies are also correct. America *is* a subversive idea. Indeed, it represents a new way to be human, and in this book we will explore what this means and whether this subversive idea is worthy of our love and allegiance.

So what is the Islamic objection to America? In conversations with Muslims from around the world, several common themes emerge. "To you we are a bunch of Ay-rabs, camel jockeys, and sand-niggers." "The only thing that we have that you care about is oil." "Americans have two things on their mind: money and sex." "Your women are whores." "In America mothers prefer to work than to take care of their children." "In our culture the parents take care of the children, and later the children take care of the parents. In America the children abandon their parents." "America used to be a Christian country. Now atheism is the official religion of the West." "Your TV shows are disgusting. You are corrupting the morals of our young people." "We don't object to how you Americans live, but now you are spreading your way of life throughout the universe." "American culture is a kind of syphilis or disease that is destroying the Islamic community. We won't let you do to us what you did to the American Indian people."

What stands out about the Islamic critique is its refreshing clarity. The Islamic thinkers cannot be counted in the ranks of the politically correct. Painful though it is to admit, they aren't entirely wrong about America either. They say that many Americans see them as a bunch of uncivilized towel heads, and this is probably true. They charge that America is a society obsessed with material gain, and who will deny this? They condemn the West as an atheistic civilization, and while they may be wrong about the extent of religious belief and practice, they are right that in the West religion has little sway over the public arena, and the West seems to have generated more unbelief than any other civilization in world history. They are disgusted by our culture, and we have to acknowledge that there is a good deal in American culture that is disgusting to normal sensibilities. They say our women are "loose," and in a sense they are right. Even their epithet for the United States, the Great Satan, is appropriate when we reflect that Satan is not a conqueror—he is a tempter. The Islamic militants fear that the idea of America is taking over their young people, breaking down allegiances to parents and religion and traditional community; this concern on their part is also justified.

The most important and influential of the Islamic critics of the West is the philosopher Sayyid Qutb.[15] Born in Egypt in 1906, Qutb became disenchanted with Arab nationalism as a weapon against Western imperialism. He became a leader and theoretician of the Muslim Brotherhood, a terrorist organization that is also one of the oldest institutions of radical Islam. Qutb argued that the worst form of colonialism—one that outlasted the formal end of European colonialism—was "intellectual and spiritual colonialism." What the Islamic world must do is destroy the influence of the West within itself, to eradicate its residue "within our feelings."

What, for Qutb, was so evil about the West? Qutb argues that from its earliest days Western civilization separated the realm of God from the realm of society. Long before the American doctrine of separation of church and state, the institutions of religion and those of government operated in separate realms and commanded separate allegiances. Consequently, Qutb argues, the realm of God and the realm of society were bound to come into conflict. And this is precisely what has happened in the West. If Athens can be taken to represent reason and science and culture, and Jerusalem can be taken to represent God and religion, then Athens has been in a constant struggle with Jerusalem. Perhaps at one point the tension could be regarded as fruitful, Qutb writes, but now the war is over, and the terrible truth is that Athens has won. Reason and science have annihilated religion. True, many people continue to profess a belief in God and go to church, but religion has ceased to have any shaping influence in society. It does not direct government or law or scientific research or culture. In short, a once-religious civilization has now been reduced to what Qutb terms *jahiliyya*—the condition of social chaos, moral diversity, sexual promiscuity, polytheism, unbelief, and idolatry that was said to characterize the Arab tribes before the advent of Islam.

Qutb's alternative to this way of life is Islam, which is much more than just a religion. Islam is not merely a set of beliefs; rather, it is a way of life based upon the divine government of the universe. The very term "Islam" means "submission" to the authority of Allah. This worldview requires that religious, economic, political, and civil society be based on the Koran, the teachings of the prophet Muhammad, and on the *sharia* or Islamic law. Islam doesn't just regulate religious belief and practice; it covers such topics as the administration of the state, the conduct of war, the making of treaties, the laws governing divorce and inheritance, as well as property rights and contracts. In short, Islam provides the whole framework for Muslim life, and in this sense it is impossible to "practice" Islam within a secular framework.

This is especially so when, as Qutb insists, the institutions of the West are antithetical to Islam. The West is a society based on freedom whereas Islam is a society based on virtue. Moreover, in Qutb's view, Western institutions are fundamentally atheistic: they are based on a clear rejection of divine authority. When democrats say that sovereignty and political authority are ultimately derived from the people, this means that the people—not God—are the rulers. So democracy is a form of idol worship. Similarly capitalism is based on the premise that the market, not God, makes final decisions of worth. Capitalism, too, is a form of idolatry or market worship. Qutb contends that since the West and Islam are based on radically different principles, there is no way that Islamic society can compromise or meet the West halfway. Either the West will prevail or Islam will prevail. What is needed, Qutb concludes, is for true-believing Muslims to recognize this and stand up for Islam against the Western infidel and those apostate Muslims who have sold out to the West for money and power. And once the critique is accepted by Muslims, the solution presents itself almost automatically. Kill the apostates. Kill the infidels.

Some Americans will find these views frightening and abhorrent, and a few people might even object to giving them so much space and taking them seriously. But I think that they must be taken seriously. Certainly they are taken seriously in the Muslim world. Moreover, Qutb is raising issues of the deepest importance: Is reason or revelation a more reliable source of truth? Does legitimate political authority come from God or from man? Which is the highest political value: freedom or virtue? These issues are central to what the West and America are all about. Qutb's critique reveals most lucidly the argument between Islam and the West at its deepest level. For this reason, it should be welcomed by thoughtful people in America and the West.

The foreign critique of America would not be so formidable if Americans were united in resisting and responding to it. Patriotism, then, would be an easy matter of "us" versus "them." But in truth there are large and influential sectors of American life that agree with many of the denunciations that come from abroad. Both on the political Left and the Right, there are people who express a strong hostility to the idea of America and the American way of life. In many quarters in the United States, we find a deep ambivalence about exporting the American system to the rest of the world. Not only do these critiques make patriotism problematic, but they also pose the question of whether an open society, where such criticisms are permitted and even encouraged, has the fortitude and the will to resist external assault. They also raise the issue of whether, if the critics are right, America is worth defending.

Conservatism is generally the party of patriotism, but in recent years, since the end of the Reagan administration, patriotism on the Right has not been much in evidence. This is not due just to post–Cold War lassitude. Many conservatives are viscerally unhappy with the current state of American society. Several right-wing leaders have pointed to the magnitude of crime, drugs, divorce, abortion, illegitimacy, and pornography as evidence that America is suffering a moral and cultural breakdown of mammoth proportions. The Reverend Jerry Falwell even suggested that the destruction of the World Trade Center was God's way of punishing America for its sinful ways. Falwell was strongly criticized, and apologized for the remark. But his cultural pessimism is echoed in the speeches of Bill Bennett, former secretary of education, and Gary Bauer, former presidential candidate and head of the Family Research Council, as well as in books such as Robert Bork's *Slouching Towards Gomorrah,* Patrick Buchanan's *The Death of the West,* and Gertrude Himmelfarb's *The De-Moralization of Society.*

How, then, can we love a society where virtue loses all her loveliness, one that has promoted what Pope John Paul II has called a "culture of death"? Some conservatives say we cannot. A few years ago the journal *First Things* argued that America had so fundamentally departed from the principles that once commanded allegiance that it was time to ask "whether conscientious citizens can no longer give moral assent to the existing regime."[16] Pat Buchanan characteristically goes further, asserting that for millions of Americans, "the good country we grew up in" has now been replaced by "a cultural wasteland and a moral sewer that are not worth living in and not worth fighting for."[17]

On the political Left, anti-Americanism has been prevalent and even fashionable at least since the Vietnam War. Admittedly a direct attack on the American homeland by Islamic fundamentalists who imprison homosexuals and refuse to educate their women was a bit too much for some, like Christopher Hitchens and David Rieff, who enrolled as supporters of the U.S. war effort. Some on the Left, too embarrassed to rationalize mass murder, and too timid to provoke the public's rage, fell prudently silent. But others could not help muttering that "America had it coming" and that "we must look at our own actions to understand the context for this attack." Columnist Barbara Ehrenreich, for example, said the United States was responsible for "the vast global inequalities in which terrorism is ultimately rooted."[18] This viewpoint was applauded at a Washington, D.C., town meeting sponsored by the

Congressional Black Caucus.[19] And on the American campus, several professors went further, blaming the United States itself for the carnage of September 11. University of Massachusetts professor Jennie Traschen suggested that America deserved what it got because throughout the world it was "a symbol of terrorism and death and fear and destruction and oppression."[20]

These strong words should not have come as a surprise. For years the left-wing opponents of globalization have carried banners in Seattle and elsewhere saying "America Must Be Stopped" and "The World Is Not For Sale." On campuses across the country, professors have been teaching their students what Columbia University scholar Edward Said recently argued: that America is a genocidal power with a "history of reducing whole peoples, countries and even continents to ruin by nothing short of holocaust."[21] Many intellectuals and activists have devoted a good deal of their adult lives to opposing what one termed "a world laid to waste by America's foreign policy, its gunboat diplomacy, its chilling disregard for non-American lives, its barbarous military interventions, its support for despotic and dictatorial regimes, its marauding multinationals, its merciless economic agenda that has munched through the economies of poor countries like a cloud of locusts."[22] Could bin Laden have put it better? If what these people say is true, then America should be destroyed.

The most serious internal critique of America comes from the political movement called multiculturalism. This group is made up of minority activists as well as of sympathetic whites who agree with their agenda. The multiculturalists are a powerful, perhaps even dominant, force in American high schools and colleges. The pervasiveness of their influence is attested in the title of a recent book by Nathan Glazer, *We Are All Multi-culturalists Now*. This group has become the shaper of the minds of American students. The multiculturalists are teaching our young people that Western civilization is defined by oppression. They present American history as an uninterrupted series of crimes visited on blacks, American Indians, Hispanics, women, and natives of the Third World. This is the theme of Howard Zinn's widely used textbook *A People's History of the United States*. Other leading scholars affirm Zinn's basic themes. Cornel West, who teaches African-American studies at Harvard, says that American society is "chronically racist, sexist and homophobic."[23] Political scientist Ali Mazrui goes further, charging that the United States has been, and continues to be, "a breeding ground for racism, exploitation and genocide."[24]

The reason America exercises such a baleful influence, multiculturalists argue, is that the American founders were slave owners and racists who established what one scholar terms "a model totalitarian society."[25] No wonder that multiculturalists are not hopeful about the future of the American experiment. In the words of historian John Hope Franklin, "We're a bigoted people and always have been. We think every other country is trying to copy us now, and if they are, God help the world."[26]

Multiculturalists insist that immigrants and minorities should not assimilate to the American mainstream, because to do so is to give up one's identity and to succumb to racism. As the influential scholar Stanley Fish puts it, "*Common values. National unity. Assimilation.* These are now the code words and phrases for an agenda that need no longer speak in the accents of the Know-Nothing party of the nineteenth century or the Ku Klux

Klan of the twentieth."[27] The multicultural objective is to encourage nonwhites in America to cultivate their separate identities and to teach white Americans to accept and even cherish these differences. For multiculturalists, diversity is the basis for American identity. As a popular slogan has it, "All we have in common is our diversity."

Multiculturalists also seek to fill white Americans with an overpowering sense of guilt and blame so that they accept responsibility for the sufferings of minorities in America and poor people in the rest of the world. One favored multicultural solution, taken up by the Reverend Jesse Jackson upon his return from the recent United Nations–sponsored World Conference on Racism in Durban, is for the American government to pay reparations for slavery to African nations and to African-Americans. "The amount we are owed," says black activist Haki Madhubuti, "is in the trillions of dollars."[28]

What we have, then, is a vivid portrait of how terrible America is and of the grave harms that it has inflicted on its people and on the world since the nation's founding. These charges of the low origins of America, and its oppressive practices, and its depraved culture, and its pernicious global influence—are they true? If so, is it possible to love our country, or are we compelled to watch her buildings knocked down and her people killed and say, in unison with her enemies, "Praise be to Allah"?

"To make us love our country," Edmund Burke wrote, "our country ought to be lovely."[29] Burke's point is that we typically love our country for the same reason that we love our children—because they are ours. Some people have kids who are intrinsically unlovable, but they love them anyway. This partiality that we all show for our own seems to be part of our tribal nature. But Burke implies that this is not the highest kind of patriotism. In the movie *The Patriot,* the hero, played by Mel Gibson, refuses to fight for America until his son is killed and his home is burned to the ground. Despite its great battle scenes, the film conveys the message that patriotism is a kind of selfishness. This would not seem to be the noblest form of patriotism, which calls us to look beyond private interests to the public benefit. As Burke suggests, the genuine patriot loves his country not only because it is his, but also because it is good.

Now, more than ever, we need this higher kind of patriotism, and it is by necessity a patriotism of the reflective sort. Reflection was not in evidence when, in the aftermath of the terrorist attack, an Arizona resident named Frank Roque fired three bullets into a Sikh gas station attendant, killing him. When the police arrived, Roque explained his actions: "I am an American." Actually, so was the man he killed, Guru Khalsa. Roque apparently thought Khalsa was a Muslim from an Arab country. Wrong man, wrong country, wrong religion. This was a rare incident, but even so it is brutish exhibitions of nativism like this one that convince some thoughtful people, like philosopher Martha Nussbaum, that attachment to any tribe or nationality is dangerous and that our moral allegiance should be to "the community of all human beings."[30]

If the only possible patriotism were based on "my country, right or wrong," then Nussbaum would be correct. If patriotism were inevitably to degenerate into the kind of blind hatred that motivated Roque, then we are better off without it. But one can make a distinction between nativism, which is based on resentment, and patriotism, which is based on love. The former is objectionable, but the latter is indispensable. Certainly America requires it now and will require it even more in the foreseeable future. Even when our initial anger toward our enemies has cooled, we still need an enduring attachment to our country to see her through the long trials ahead. America desperately needs the love of her citizens, for what she is and for what she might become.

A patriotism of this sort—a thoughtful and affirming patriotism—must necessarily be based on an examination of first principles. The need for this approach was illustrated by an American radio show host who recently erupted, "I don't know why those crazy Muslims want to fight with us. They believe in Allah this, and Allah that, and they don't realize that we don't give a damn. So why can't we just agree to disagree?" The reason, of course, is that *agreeing to disagree* is a liberal principle, and it is liberalism itself that is being disputed here. The procedural liberalism that we are so used to invoking—which presupposes that liberal mechanisms like free speech and equal rights are the best way of organizing society—is ineffective against those who do not believe that these are self-evident goods and who insist that religious truth and virtue have higher claims. We have to show why our society is a moral improvement on theirs, and this is neither an obvious nor an easy task.

I feel that I am in a unique position to write about this subject. I am a native of India who grew up in Bombay and came to the United States as an exchange student in the late 1970s. Since I spent the first part of my life in a different society, I am able to see the United States from the outside and to identify unique aspects of American society that seem completely unremarkable to the natives. This may be called the "Tocqueville advantage," although, in invoking it, I am by no means comparing myself to Tocqueville. Visiting America in the 1830s, Tocqueville declared that he had encountered "a distinct species of mankind." Tocqueville was especially struck by the average American's "inordinate love of material gratification." At the same time, Tocqueville detected a restlessness of soul that afflicted even the most fortunate and prosperous families. Tocqueville observed that, by contrast with Europeans, Americans exhibited a high degree of civic activism and religious fervor. Tocqueville further remarked that Americans were fierce egalitarians who, despite differences of income and status, refused to bow and scrape before anybody.[31]

These are perceptive observations, and most of them are true today. But a great deal has also changed since Tocqueville came here, and the United States displays some new distinguishing characteristics. I am impressed at the fact that Americans cannot fight a war and say they are doing it for strategic advantage or for oil; they have to be convinced, or to convince themselves, that they are fighting to expel a tyrant, or to secure democracy, or to ensure human rights. In other societies there are multiple measures of social recognition, such as family background, education, caste, and so on; in the United States, it pretty much comes down to how much money you have. Even so, "old money" carries very little prestige in America: all it means is that your grandfather was a robber baron or a bootlegger. As a frequent speaker at American companies, I am struck by the ease with which Palestinians and

Jews, Hindus and Muslims, Turks and Armenians, all work together in apparent disregard of the bitter historical grievances that have shattered their communities of origin. Elsewhere in the world the poor aspire to middle-class respectability, but in the United States the wealthy seek to dress and act like middle-class people, or even like bums. American children seem to believe quite literally that you can "be whatever you want to be," implausible though this seems to people in other places. American parents seem unnaturally eager to befriend their children and to treat them as equals, yet the children seem firmly convinced that they are far wiser than their elders. Young people in the United States "go away to college" and typically never return home to live. In many other countries this would be regarded as abandoning one's offspring. Americans are the friendliest people you will encounter, but they have few friends. Most people in the United States do not believe in idleness and pursue even leisure with a kind of strenuous effort. There are very weird people in America, but nobody seems struck or bothered by the amount of weirdness. In many countries old people believe their life is over and pretty much wait to die, while in America people in their seventies pursue the pleasures of life, including remarriage and sexual gratification, with a zeal that I find unnerving. While the funeral is a standard public ceremony in most countries, funerals are a very rare public sight in America, and no one likes to go to them. It seems that Americans don't really die: they just disappear. The significance of some of these cultural peculiarities will be explored later in this book.

Another reason I feel especially qualified to write this book is that I have the background and credentials to evaluate the various accusations that are launched against the United States and the West. Having been raised in a country that was colonized by the West for several hundred years, I have a good vantage point to assess how Western civilization has harmed or helped the peoples of the non-Western world. As a "person of color" who has lived in the United States for more than twenty years, and having devoted a decade to studying issues of race and ethnicity, I am competent to address such questions as what it is like to be a nonwhite person in America, what this country owes its indigenous minorities, and whether immigrants can maintain their ethnic identity and still "become American."

I became a U.S. citizen myself in 1991. I took the oath that fateful day, and over the years my identification with America has deepened to the point that I truly feel that I have "become an American." This phrase has become common enough that we don't give it a thought, and yet it is fraught with meaning. An American could come to India and stay for forty years, perhaps even taking Indian citizenship, but he could not "become Indian." Indians would not consider such a person Indian, nor would it be possible for him to think of himself in that way. The reason is that being Indian, like being German or Swedish or Iranian, is entirely a matter of birth and blood. You become Indian by having Indian parents.

In America, by contrast, millions of people come from all over the world, and over time most of them come to think of themselves as Americans. Sometimes their children and grandchildren forget where they came from, or stop caring. Whatever their origins, these people have somehow, like me, "become American." Their experience suggests that becoming American is less a function of birth or blood and more a function of embracing a set of ideas. It is only for this reason that terms like "un-American" and "anti-American" make sense. You could not accuse someone of being "un-German" or "un-Pakistani." They would not know what you were talking about.

I believe that over the years I have developed an understanding of the central idea that makes America great, and I have seen the greatness of America reflected in my life. At the same time I take seriously the issues raised by the critics of America. I know that they are onto something as well. In recent years my enthusiasm about America has been shaken by the experience of parenthood. As the father of a seven-year-old girl, I have come to realize how much more difficult it is to raise her well in America than it would be for me and my wife to raise her in India. We are constantly battling to shield our daughter from toxic influences in American culture that threaten to destroy her innocence. And even as I seek to insulate her from those influences, I am not sure that I can. This is a battle that I know I might lose. Why, I sometimes ask myself, do I stay in America?

I mention these details to make the point that I feel the force of the arguments for and against America, because they play out in my own life. This is a book that seeks to integrate my research and study about America with my personal experience of American life. It is a book that faces the harshest critics of America and the West, but concludes that those critics are wrong. They are missing something of great significance about Western civilization and about the American way of life. So for all my qualms, I will not be returning to India. I know that my daughter will have a better life if I stay. I don't mean just that she will be better off; I mean that her life is likely to have greater depth, meaning, and fulfillment in the United States than it would in any other country. I have come to appreciate that there is something great and noble about America, and in this book I intend to say what that is.

TWO CHEERS
FOR COLONIALISM
How the West Prevailed

Whatever happens, we have got
The Maxim gun, and they have not.

—HILAIRE BELLOC

WE LIVE IN A WORLD THAT HAS BEEN DECISIVELY
shaped by Western civilization. Travel to virtually
any part of the globe, and the signs and symbols of
Western dominance are omnipresent. In India, for example, the
houses of Parliament are divided into the *Lok Sabha*—a lower or
"people's house"—and the *Rajya Sabha*—an upper or "royal
house." India has a parliamentary system of government that
closely mirrors that of the British. Moreover, the Indian business
community speaks English and begins its day with another Western institution—the daily newspaper. Indian cities now have muse-
ums, which did not exist in ancient India and have been replicated
from the West. People go to work in Western suits and ties, even
though this attire seems utterly unsuited to India's hot climate.

Even India's army wears Western uniforms and uses the same ranking hierarchy as the West. India has universities modeled on the Western system, which emphasize science and technology and confer degrees on solemn Indian graduates who wear a Western medieval uniform—caps and gowns—for the purpose. In short, the configuration of life in India, as in most countries, is in crucial respects determined by Western civilization.

Yet tens of millions of American students do not know this. When I tell high-school and college students about it in my lectures, they profess ignorance, even indignation. The reason is that they have been getting a very different message from their professors. "The Indians are being forced to live like this," they insist. "It is what the British inflicted on them." Well, perhaps; but the British left India in 1947, and India became free. The Indians could easily have cast off their suits and ties and returned to their native garb. They had the option of returning to ancient tribal modes of government. The Indians could have outlawed the English language and required all education to be in Hindustani or one of the native dialects. But the Indians did not do any of these things. They decided on their own, and for their benefit, to continue doing many of the things that they had learned from the British.

This thought upsets many American students. The reason for their distress is that what our young people know is largely a product of multicultural education, which teaches them to despise Western civilization. One of the central premises of multiculturalism is that Western civilization is not superior to, or better than, any other civilization. To think this, in the multicultural view, is to be guilty of racism. Against this doctrine of cultural superiority, multiculturalists insist that all cultures are basically equal, each culture is an adaptation to its own unique environment, and no culture is better or worse than, superior or inferior to, any other.

A few years ago the novelist Saul Bellow reportedly made the remark, "Show me the Proust of the Papuans, the Tolstoy of the Zulus, and I will read him." Bellow's comment was greeted with a universal cry of outrage. As one Ivy League professor put it, Bellow's statement was "astoundingly racist." But why? Bellow was not suggesting that the Papuans were incapable of producing a Proust, or the Zulus a Tolstoy. He was merely saying that, as far as he knew, they hadn't. But Bellow's sin was to imply that some cultures, and specifically Western culture, might have contributed more to the dining table of civilization than others. This violated the multicultural premise of the equality of all cultures.

Another example: in the early 1990s, I attended a meeting of a historical society at which academicians were virtually coming to blows over the question of whether Columbus "discovered" America or whether he merely "encountered" America. An odd subject for fisticuffs, certainly. But beneath the semantic dispute was a larger issue. You see, the notion of discovery implies a subject and an object, as in "Fleming discovered penicillin." By contrast "encounter" is a more neutral term that implies a meeting on a plane of equality. The historians who objected to the term "discovery" were trying to camouflage the fact that it was Columbus and his ships that ventured out and landed on the shores of the Americas, and not American Indians who landed on the shores of Europe.

If one begins with the multicultural premise that all cultures are equal, then the world as it is makes very little sense. After all, we live in a world where, by virtually any measure of achievement or success, some cultures are advanced and others are backward. To take one measure of success that everybody seems to want— economic development—it is obvious that the West is vastly ahead of everyone else. There is simply no comparison between, say, the per capita income of Europe and America and that of the nations of sub-Saharan Africa. If sub-Saharan Africa were to sink into the ocean tomorrow, the world economy would be largely unaffected.[1] We could use other measures of civilizational achievement, but the result would remain largely the same. The prevalence of poverty, repression, civil war, AIDS, and other horrors recently persuaded UN secretary general Kofi Annan to term sub-Saharan Africa "a cocktail of disasters." Hierarchy, not equality, appears to be the governing principle for the cultures of the world as they are now.

Multiculturalists do not so much deny this as object to it on moral grounds. In their view, to rank Western civilization at the top, to give priority to the West, to establish a curriculum focused on the West, is to be guilty of "Eurocentrism." The term "Eurocentrism" simply means placing Europe at the center of things, and it sounds like a pretty narrow and arrogant way to view the world. But of course if we are trying to describe the world in which we live, indeed the modern world of the past few centuries, then it is entirely accurate to focus on Europe, to place Western civilization at the center. Indeed, it was the West, expanding outward, which found and conquered and defined the rest of the world. For example, "Asia," "Africa," and the "Middle East" did not exist before Westerners came up with those names and a geography that divided up the planet in that way. "India" was made up of an assortment of local kingdoms before it developed—through its relationship to the West—national boundaries and eventually a sense of national identity.

The "Eurocentric" approach seems entirely justified when you consider that Western civilization has dominated the world for nearly five centuries. Within the West, admittedly, the center of power has shifted. Inside the competing orbit of the West, the Portuguese first had the upper hand, then the Spanish, then the French, and then the English. Even so, never in the past few hundred years has the leadership position slipped out of the hands of the West. On the contrary, the West became more and more influential to the point that, a century ago, in the early part of the twentieth century, nearly 85 percent of the real estate on the planet was under the control and supervision of Western civilization.[2] It was the heyday of colonialism.

In avidly seeking to downplay Western political, economic, military, and cultural superiority, advocates of multiculturalism emphasize that all cultures are on an equal plane and are equally worthy of study. Thus the multicultural curriculum treats in great detail the traditional religions and customs of non-Western cultures, even though many of those customs and mores are on the way out in those cultures. This fact was comically illustrated for me recently when I was watching on television a replay of the heavyweight title fight between Muhammad Ali and George Foreman. It was held in the 1970s in the African nation of Zaire, and somewhat insensitively billed as the "Rumble in the Jungle." Both Ali and Foreman studied their African roots, in order to win the support of the crowd and establish a psychological edge against the other. When their plane arrived, out came Ali, out came Foreman, and both were impressively regaled in traditional African outfits: headdresses, dashikis, and so on. But there to greet them on the tarmac were several hundred Africans *in suits*, looking a little puzzled at this clear case of multiculturalism gone awry.

My point is that American multiculturalists are giving our students museumized portraits of non-Western cultures even as those cultures have moved, and continue to move, rapidly in the direction of the West. Thus American students are getting a false picture. They are not being prepared to face the world as it is, a world that is shaped and dominated by Western civilization.

Why did Western civilization become so dominant in the modern era? How did this massive transformation of the world begin? This important question is rendered all the more provocative by the realization that for most of human history, other civilizations have proven far more advanced than the West: more advanced in learning, in wealth, in exploration, in inventions, and in cultural sophistication and works of the mind. We can see this clearly by taking an imaginative leap back in time to A.D. 1500, when "the West" as we know it now was just starting to emerge.

In A.D. 1500 there were several civilizations dotting the globe, and two of them stood out in resplendence: the civilization of China and the civilization of the Arab-Islamic world. During the Ming dynasty, the wealth, knowledge, and power of China astonished all those who came into contact with it. Chinese astronomers knew more about eclipses and heavenly orbits than anyone else at the time. The Chinese were responsible for inventions of surpass-

ing importance: printing, gunpowder, and the compass. In the fifteenth century the Chinese sent a fleet of ships, the largest and
most sophisticated of their kind, to explore the shores of Africa,
India, and other countries. At home, the Chinese ruling class
presided over an empire distinguished by its size and cohesion.
Confucian philosophy gave a kind of moral and intellectual unity
to Chinese civilization. The Chinese had a merit system of government appointments when most of the world operated on traditional systems of nepotism and patronage. Chinese society
showed a refinement in porcelain work, in silk embroidery, and in
social refinement, that no other society could match. No wonder
the Chinese emperors regarded themselves as the "sons of
Heaven" and their part of the world as the center of the universe.[3]

Equally impressive in the year 1500 were the achievements of
Islamic civilization. Starting in the seventh century, the Islamic
empire spread rapidly until it sprawled across three continents:
Europe, Asia, and Africa. The Muslims unified their enormous
empire around a single faith, Islam, and a single language, Arabic.
The Islamic world enjoyed a flourishing economy, enriched by
trade with India and the Far East, and a largely uniform system of
laws. The Muslims built spectacular cities—Baghdad, Damascus,
Cairo, Istanbul, Seville, Granada—distinguished by architectural
and literary splendor. Islamic literature and thought exhibited a
richness, variety, and complexity that far surpassed that of Europe
at the time. Islam produced great men of learning, such as Ibn
Sinha (Avicenna), Ibn Rushd (Averroes), Ibn Khaldun, al-Ghazali,
al-Farabi, and al-Kindi. Indeed, much of Greco-Roman knowledge, including the works of Aristotle, that had been lost in Europe
during the Dark Ages was preserved in the Islamic world. It is no

exaggeration to write, in the words of historian David Landes, that during this period "Islam was Europe's teacher."[4]

Nothing could compare to China and the Islamic empire, but there were other civilizations in the world in the year 1500. There was the civilization of India, renowned for its spiritual depth as the original home of two of the world's great religions, Hindusim and Buddhism, and also famous for its wealth and mathematical learning. In Africa there were the kingdoms of Ghana, Mali, and Songhay, which were large, orderly, and rich in gold. Finally in the Americas there were the Aztec and Inca civilizations. Despite their reputation for brutality and human sacrifice, these were impressive for their architecture, social organization, and city planning.

Western civilization—then called Christendom—was a relative backwater. Mired in the Dark Ages, Christendom was characterized by widespread ignorance, poverty, and incessant clashes between warring tribes and between kings and the Church. Indeed, Islamic writers who encountered the West in the late Middle Ages describe it as remote, uninteresting, and primitive. A Muslim traveler described Europeans as "more like beasts than like men. They lack keenness of understanding, and clarity of intelligence, and are overcome by ignorance and apathy, lack of discernment and stupidity." Another Muslim writer gives an account of the state of European medicine. He tells of a knight who came to a European physician complaining of an abscess on his leg; the physician seized an ax and chopped off the leg with one blow "and the man died at once." Bernard Lewis finds in such Muslim writings "the same note of amused disdain as we sometimes find among European travelers in Africa and Asia many centuries later."[5]

How, then, did this relatively impoverished, backward civilization accumulate so much economic, political, and military power that it was able to conquer and subdue all the other cultures of the world put together? There are two popular theories to answer this question. The first is the "environmental" school, and its thesis is conveyed by the title of a recent book, *The Geography Behind History*. According to this view, cultures are the product of location and natural resources, and whether a culture develops or remains stagnant depends on such factors as the availability of mineral resources, climate, proximity to rivers, and such. Africa, for example, is much larger than Europe but has a shorter navigable coastline, and therefore it seems to enjoy fewer possibilities for commerce. The most eloquent expression of the environmental argument is given by Jared Diamond in his best-selling book *Guns, Germs, and Steel*. Diamond argues that Europe enjoyed immense natural advantages in prehistoric times that gave it a "head start" over the other cultures of the world.[6]

The environmental thesis does help to account for the origins of the earliest human civilizations. The flourishing of these civilizations did, in fact, depend decisively on access to water. Thus the civilization of the Fertile Crescent was made possible by the Tigris and Euphrates Rivers. Not for nothing has ancient Egypt been termed "the gift of the Nile." Other ancient civilizations developed on the banks of the Indus River in India and the Yellow River in China. But beyond this the environmental thesis in general, and Diamond's arguments in particular, are useless in explaining the triumph of the West. After all, if Diamond is right that Europe enjoyed a natural advantage from ancient times, then why did this lead not become manifest until modern times? For more than a thousand years—say between A.D. 500 and A.D. 1500—the West was a civilizational laggard and showed no signs of becoming the world's dominant civilization. As we have seen, all bets were on China and the Islamic world. For the success of the West in the past five hundred years in "coming from behind" to take over the world, Diamond and the environmental school have no plausible explanation.

Despite its intellectual limitations, the environmental school retains its appeal among critics of the West because it attributes the civilizational superiority of Europe largely to chance. But there is a second, even more popular, explanation within the anti-Western camp. According to this view, the reason that Western civilization became dominant in the past five hundred years is because it is evil. Oppression—and specifically the crimes of ethnocentrism, colonialism, imperialism, and racism—is said to be the key to Western success. This may be called the school of "oppression theory," and its thesis may be summarized in the statement that the West grew rich and powerful by beating up everybody else and taking their stuff.

Oppression theory is highly favored by advocates of multiculturalism because it allows them to account for the disjunction between their dogma of cultural equality and the reality that the cultures of the world are far from equal. Multiculturalists reason that because all cultures are equal, existing inequality is undoubtedly the consequence of some cultures oppressing others. A few years ago Jesse Jackson led a group of protesters at Stanford University with banners advertising the sins of the West. Jackson and the demonstrators chanted, "Hey hey, ho ho, Western culture's got to go." A more scholarly version of the oppression thesis can be found in the works of Edward Said, particularly in his influential study *Orientalism* and his more recent book *Culture and Imperialism*.

Outside the West, oppression theory is also popular among Third World intellectuals like the Marxist scholar Samir Amin, author of *Eurocentrism*. Another Marxist, Walter Rodney, blames European colonialism for "draining African wealth and making it impossible to develop more rapidly the resources of the continent."[7] A similar note is struck by the African writer Chinweizu, who offers the following explanation for African underdevelopment: "White hordes have sallied forth from their western homelands to assault, loot, occupy, rule, and exploit the world. Even now, the fury of their expansionist assault upon the rest of us has not abated."[8]

Perhaps the most forceful exponent of oppression theory is the anticolonial writer Frantz Fanon. Fanon writes, "European opulence has been founded on slavery. The well-being and progress of Europe have been built up with the sweat and the dead bodies of Negroes, Arabs, Indians and the yellow races."[9] In recent years Fanon's oppression thesis has been taken up with a vengeance by many in the Islamic world. Islamic radicals are familiar with, and frequently cite, Fanon. And Muslim devotees of his work go considerably beyond the bin Laden circle. Even many Muslims who do not condone terrorism seem firmly to believe that they are poor because the West is rich, that somehow the West is to blame for their poverty and misery.

The multicultural remedy is a simple one. Multiculturalists call upon the West to publicly atone for its crimes and pay up. Reparations for slavery is the favored approach. Jesse Jackson strongly supports the idea.[10] African-American activist Randall Robinson advocated it in a recent book, black lawyers like Johnnie Cochran and Charles Ogletree are drawing up a legal strategy to promote it through the courts, and members of the Congressional Black Caucus have taken up the political cudgels to convince the U.S. government to go along. For many Third World and Islamic activists, reparations are not enough. For them, the crimes of the West provide a justification for violence. Fanon himself advocated such violence—"The native is an oppressed person whose permanent dream is to become the persecutor"—and his battle cry has been taken up by Islamic radicals who have found in it an added pretext for *jihad*.

It must be granted that if the wealth and success of the West are the product of distinctive Western evils such as slavery and colonialism, if they amount to nothing more than "stolen goods" pirated from the rest of the world, then the West should atone for its crimes and pay reparations to those it has robbed. One could even argue that, under such circumstances, some form of violent retaliation against an unrepentant West is both understandable and justified. The question we must face, therefore, is whether the advocates of oppression theory are right.

It is impossible to deny that ethnocentrism, colonialism, and slavery are all part of the history of the West. What we have to determine, however, is whether there is anything intrinsically Western about these practices, and whether the West's participation in them is the cause of its wealth and success.

First, ethnocentrism. This notion that "our way is the best way" and that "we are better than everyone else" is certainly part of the legacy of Europe going all the way back to the ancient

Greeks. The ancient Greeks distinguished between the civilized and the barbarians, and found themselves to be the most civilized people in the world. Later the medieval Christians drew their own distinction: between the believer and the infidel. Still later the champions of the West drew another line of demarcation, this time between the white man, who was held to be superior, and the yellow and brown and black men, who were held to be inferior.

When we look to other cultures, however, we find that there is nothing distinctively Western about ethnocentrism. It is present in abundance beyond Western shores. The Chinese, for instance, believed themselves to be the Middle Kingdom, the center of the universe. They were so convinced of this that Western visitors like the Jesuit Matteo Ricci could persuade the Chinese court to consider Western maps only when they were redrawn to place China at the center of the world. And just as the Chinese emperors considered themselves emissaries of heaven, so too the Indian kings called themselves *Chakravarty Rajas,* which literally means "universal sovereigns." Of course Islam resembled Christianity in believing itself in possession of the whole revealed truth, with everyone else consigned to ignorance and darkness.

These arrogant proclamations may be understandable when they are made by the representatives of great civilizations, but anthropologists like Ruth Benedict show that even the world's most primitive tribes are ethnocentric. Indeed, it is frequently the case that the less developed a tribe, the more ethnocentric it is. Groups of people that can barely feed themselves, that have still not discovered the wheel, whose counting does not go above the number two, still consider themselves the greatest and favored by the gods and their way of life the best way. What this research confirms is that ethnocentrism is universal, and it is not necessarily substantiated by civilizational achievement.

What is distinctively Western is not ethnocentrism but a profound and highly beneficial effort to transcend ethnocentrism. Only in the West has there been a consistent willingness to question the identification of the good with one's own way. Even the Greek philosophers, who scorned the primitivism of the barbarians, admitted that non-Greeks were capable of civilization. In his *Education of Cyrus,* the Greek writer Xenophon located his ideal regime not in Greece but in Persia. Greek thinkers from Herodotus to Aristotle showed an inexhaustible interest in other cultures, and this curiosity about others, as well as a desire to learn from them, became a staple of Western civilization. Alongside ethnocentrism, the West has long entertained a fascination with the other, and even a belief in the superiority of the other. It was the West, after all, which invented the notion of the "noble savage." We take this curiosity so much for granted that it surprises many to learn that other cultures historically have not shared it.

The truth, however, is that throughout its history Western civilization has gained immensely from its absorption of the ideas and inventions of other cultures. From the Muslims the West recovered parts of its own lost Greco-Roman heritage. Muslim thinkers like Ibn Sinha, Ibn Rushd, and al-Farabi had a powerful impact on the philosophical debates in the West. From the Hindus the West learned its numeral system, including the number zero and the concept of negative numbers. The Hindus developed this system, but it was brought to Europe by the Arabs, and thus the Europeans erroneously called it "Arabic numerals." Despite the misnomer, it seems evident that without Arabic numerals the West could not have made the progress it subsequently did in mathematics and science. Equations and calculus are hard, if not impossible, to perform with Roman numerals. As Thomas Sowell wryly observes, today Roman numerals are only used for naming kings and Super Bowls.

This example shows that civilizational development does not always go to the group that invents things. It frequently goes to the people who are able to take the inventions and run with them. The Chinese were responsible for inventing printing, gunpowder, and the compass. They knew all these things since the eleventh century. Yet these inventions were closely held by the Chinese court, and they had a very limited impact on Chinese society. Printing, for example, was mainly used by the emperor to issue official documents. By contrast, once the West learned about these inventions they had a convulsive, transforming impact on European society. Gunpowder revolutionized Western warfare and gave European nations the means to impose their will on other peoples. Printing made possible the Gutenberg Bible and the Reformation. It allowed the spread of literacy and created the conditions for the rise of democracy. The compass helped the West develop navigational resources to venture forth to the far corners of the world, inaugurating the new age that we call modernity.

But if the West has shown itself willing and eager to learn from other cultures, this attitude has not been reciprocated until recent times by other cultures. In the Islamic empire, for instance, a prevailing view was that Muslims have nothing to learn from other people. This attitude may strike us as the provincialism of the lowly and the ignorant, but in fact it was shared by many of the most sophisticated minds of Islam. For instance, Ibn Khaldun—

the preeminent Muslim historian of the Middle Ages—writes a universal history called *The Muqaddimah* but shows absolutely no interest in what is going on outside Islamic civilization. "God knows better what exists there."[11] Even more striking is that, in subsequent centuries, when the leading figures of the Muslim world heard about the raging debates in Europe over democracy and popular sovereignty and human rights, they ignored them. Muslims had access to political and scientific works from the West, but they never bothered to translate them into Arabic. The Renaissance, the Enlightenment, and the Scientific Revolution passed without notice in the Islamic world. This self-imposed isolation has had immense consequences both for Islam and for the West, consequences that we are living with today.

The Chinese were, if anything, even more ethnocentric than the Muslims. By all accounts China, not Europe, should have dominated the age of exploration. Early in the fifteenth century, the Chinese admiral Zheng He (also known as Cheng Ho) inaugurated a series of voyages to Southeast Asia, India, the Persian Gulf, and the coast of Africa. The Chinese had the best astronomy, the best cartography, the best navigational skill, and the best built ships in the world. Even so, they made several voyages to other countries and then stopped.[12] Chinese exploration came to an abrupt end around 1433, more than half a century before Columbus took his epochal voyage to the Americas.

Why, then, did the Chinese quit? One clue is provided by a Chinese ship that arrived on the Indian shore in search of animals for the Chinese zoo. The expedition yielded a giraffe, which caused quite a sensation at the Chinese court. But no other Chinese ships came to India, presumably because the needs of the Chinese zoo were satisfied. In general, the Chinese went abroad not to learn from other people—a prospect they found impossible—but rather to demonstrate their own greatness and to find people to pay tribute to their civilization and to their emperor. Once their vanity was appeased they decided to forgo the expense of foreign travel, and they called the whole thing to a halt. Zheng He has been called the Chinese Columbus, but he is more accurately termed "the man who could have been Columbus." Daniel Boorstin suggests that the exploits of Zheng He were anomalous; a more appropriate symbol of Chinese psychology is the Great Wall, built to keep the Chinese in and everyone else out.[13]

If ethnocentrism is not Western, what about colonialism? Well, colonialism is also not a unique characteristic of the West. My native country of India, for example, was ruled by the British for more than two centuries, and many of my fellow Indians are still smarting about that. What they often forget, however, is that before the British came the Indians were invaded and conquered by the Persians, by the Afghans, by Alexander the Great, by the Arabs, by the Mongols, and by the Turks. Depending on how you count, the British were the eighth or ninth colonial power to invade India. The English were merely the latest installment in a series of conquerors who forced their way onto Indian soil since ancient times. Indeed, ancient India was itself the product of the Aryan people who came from the north and subjugated the dark-skinned indigenous people.

Those who identify colonialism and empire only with the West either have no sense of history or have forgotten about the Persian empire, the Macedonian empire, the Islamic empire, the

Mongol empire, the Chinese empire, and the Aztec and Inca empires in the Americas. Shouldn't the Arabs be paying reparations for their destruction of the Byzantine and Persian empires? Come to think of it, shouldn't the Byzantine and Persian people also pay reparations to the descendants of the people they subjugated? And while we're at it, shouldn't the Muslims reimburse the Spaniards for their seven-hundred-year rule? As the example of Islamic Spain suggests, the people of the West have participated in the game of conquest not only as the perpetrator, but also as the victims. Ancient Greece, for example, was conquered by Rome, and the Roman Empire itself was destroyed by the invasions of Huns, Vandals, Lombards, and Visigoths from northern Europe. America, as we all know, was itself a colony of England before its war of independence; England, before that, was subjugated and ruled by the Norman kings from France. Those of us living today are taking on a large project if we are going to settle upon a rule of social justice based upon figuring out whose ancestors did what to whom.

Perhaps it is not colonialism but slavery that is distinctively Western. Actually, no. Slavery has existed in all known civilizations. In his study *Slavery and Social Death,* the West Indian sociologist Orlando Patterson writes, "Slavery has existed from the dawn of human history, in the most primitive of human societies and in the most civilized. There is no region on earth that has not at some time harbored the institution."[14] A brief survey of the nations of the world confirms this. The Sumerians and Babylonians practiced slavery, as did the ancient Egyptians. The Chinese, the Indians, and the Arabs all had slaves. Slavery was widespread in Greece and Rome, and also in sub-Saharan Africa.

American Indians practiced slavery long before Columbus set one foot on this continent.

If slavery is not distinctively Western, what is? The movement to end slavery! Abolition is an exclusively Western institution. The historian J. M. Roberts writes, "No civilization once dependent on slavery has ever been able to eradicate it, except the Western."[15] Of course, slaves in every society don't want to be slaves. The history of slavery is full of incidents of runaways, slave revolts, and so on. But typically slaves were captured in warfare, and if they got away they were perfectly happy to take other people as slaves.

Never in the history of the world, outside of the West, has a group of people eligible to be slave owners mobilized against the institution of slavery. This distinctive Western attitude is reflected by Abraham Lincoln: "As I would not be a slave, so I would not be a master."[16] Lincoln doesn't want to be a slave—that's not surprising—but he doesn't want to be a master either. He and many other people were willing to expend considerable treasure, and ultimately blood, to get rid of slavery not for themselves, but for other people. The uniqueness of this Western approach is confirmed by the little-known fact that African chiefs, who profited from the slave trade, sent delegations to the West to protest the abolition of slavery.[17] And it is important to realize that the slaves were not in a position to secure freedom for themselves. The descendants of African slaves owe their freedom to the exertions of white strangers, not to the people of Africa who betrayed them and sold them.

Surely all of this is relevant to the reparations debate. A trenchant observation on the matter was offered years ago by Muhammad Ali, shortly after his defeat of George Foreman for the heavyweight title. Upon returning to the United States, Ali was asked by a reporter, "Champ, what did you think of Africa?" Ali replied, "Thank God my granddaddy got on that boat!" There is a mischievous pungency to this remark that is entirely in keeping with Ali's character. But there is also a profound meaning behind Ali's words that I would like to explain by starting with a context more familiar to me, the context of colonialism.

While I was a young boy growing up in India, I noticed that my grandfather, who had lived under British colonialism, was instinctively and habitually antiwhite. He wasn't just against the English, he was generally against the white man. For him, the white man was basically a scoundrel, and if he ever came across a white man, he had a way of showing that the seemingly innocuous fellow was actually up to no good. When I first proposed the idea of going to America, he dissuaded me. "You should stay away from that place," he said. "It's full of white people." I realized that he had an animus that I did not share. This puzzled me: why did he and I feel so differently?

Only years later, after a great deal of experience and a fair amount of study, did the answer finally hit me. The reason for our difference of perception was that colonialism had been pretty bad for him, but pretty good for me. Another way to put it was that colonialism had injured those who lived under it, but paradoxically it proved beneficial to their descendants. Much as it chagrins me to admit it—and much as it will outrage many Third World intellectuals for me to say it—my life would have been much worse had the British never ruled India.

How is this possible? Virtually everything that I am, what I do, and my deepest beliefs, all are the product of a worldview that was brought to India by colonialism. I am a writer, and I write in English. My ability to do this, and to reach a world market, is indebted to the British. If not for them, I might still be a writer (actually this is extremely doubtful, but for reasons given later), but I would write in a local language (Konkani or Marathi) and reach a very limited audience. My understanding of technology, which allows me, like so many Indians, to function successfully in the modern world, was entirely the product of a Western education that came to India as a result of the British. So also my beliefs in freedom of expression, in self-government, in equality of rights under the law, and in the universal principle of human dignity—they are all the product of Western civilization.

I am not suggesting that it was the intention of the colonialists to give all these wonderful gifts to the Indians. Admittedly some apologists for colonialism, such as Macaulay and Kipling, wrote as if the British endured a "white man's burden" to share civilization with the lesser peoples. More candidly, Lord Lugard spoke of colonialism's "dual mandate": to help the local people *and* to benefit the ruling power. In practice, of course, the colonialists routinely subordinated the first objective to the second. Colonialism was not based on philanthropy; it was a form of conquest and rule. The English came to India to govern, and they were not primarily interested in the development of the natives, whom they viewed as picturesque savages. It is impossible to measure, or overlook, the enormous pain and humiliation that was inflicted by the rulers over their long period of occupation. Understandably the Indians chafed under this yoke. Toward the end of the British reign in India Mahatma Gandhi was asked, "What do you think of Western civilization?" He replied, "I think it would be a good idea."

Despite their suspect motives and bad behavior, however, the British needed a certain amount of infrastructure in order to govern India effectively. So they built roads, and shipping docks, and railway tracks, and irrigation systems, and government buildings. Then the British realized that they needed courts of law to adjudicate disputes that went beyond local systems of dispensing justice. And so the English legal system was introduced, with all its procedural novelties, such as "innocent until proven guilty." The English also had to educate the Indians in order to communicate with them and to train them to be civil servants in the empire. Thus Indian children were exposed to Shakespeare, and Dickens, and Hobbes, and Locke. In this way the Indians began to encounter new words and new ideas that were unmentioned in their ancestral culture: "liberty," "sovereignty," "rights," and so on.

This brings me to the greatest benefit that the British provided to the Indians: they taught them the language of freedom. Once again, it was not the objective of the English to encourage rebellion. But by exposing Indians to the ideas of the West, they did. The Indian leaders were the product of Western civilization. Gandhi studied in England and South Africa, Nehru was a product of Harrow and Cambridge. This exposure was not entirely to the good. Nehru, for example, who became India's first prime minister after independence, was highly influenced by Fabian socialism through the teachings of Harold Laski. The result was that India had a mismanaged socialist economy for a generation. But my broader point is that the champions of Indian independence acquired the principles and the language and even the strategies of liberation from the civilization of their oppressors. This was true not just of India but also of other Asian and African countries that broke free of the European yoke.

My conclusion is that *against their intentions* the colonialists brought things to India that have immeasurably enriched the lives of the descendants of colonialism. Colonialism was the transmission belt that brought to India the blessings of Western civilization. It was a harsh regime for those who lived under it, to be sure. My grandfather would have a hard time giving even one cheer for colonialism. As for me, I cannot manage three, but I am quite willing to grant two. So here it is: two cheers for colonialism! Maybe you will now see why I am not going to be sending an invoice for reparations to Tony Blair.

Back to Muhammad Ali: I understand him to be making the same point. Slavery was a grave moral crime that inflicted incalculable harm to the slaves. But the slaves are dead, and the truth is that their descendants are better off as a result of slavery. Jesse Jackson is vastly better off because his ancestors were enslaved than he would have been if that had never happened. If not for slavery, Jackson and others like him would be living in Somalia or Ethiopia or Nigeria. The enormous improvement in their condition can be verified by simply asking them whether they would consider moving to one of those places. As the African-American writer Zora Neale Hurston bluntly put it, "Slavery is the price I paid for civilization, and that is worth all that I have paid through my ancestors for it."[18]

I realize that in saying these things I am opening the door for my critics, and the incorrigible enemies of the West, to say that I am justifying colonialism and slavery. This is the purest nonsense. What I am doing is pointing out a historical fact: despite the corrupt and self-serving motives of their practitioners, the institutions of colonialism and slavery proved to be the mechanism that brought millions of nonwhite people into the orbit of Western freedom.

☆☆☆

It makes no sense to claim that the West grew rich and powerful by taking everybody else's stuff for a simple reason: there wasn't very much to take. "Oh yes there was," the retort often comes. "The Europeans stole the raw material to build their civilization. They stole rubber from Malaya, and cocoa from West Africa, and tea from India." But as economic historian Peter Bauer points out, before British rule, there *were* no rubber trees in Malaya, nor cocoa trees in West Africa, nor tea in India. The British brought the rubber tree to Malaya from South America. They brought tea to India from China. And they taught the Africans to grow cocoa, a crop the native people had previously never heard of.[19] None of this is to deny that when the colonialists could exploit native resources, they did. But this larceny cannot possibly account for the enormous gap in economic, political, and military power that opened up between the rest of the world and the West.

What, then, is the real source of that power? I want to suggest that the reason the West became the dominant civilization in the modern era is because it invented three institutions: science, democracy, and capitalism. These institutions did not exist anywhere else in the world, nor did they exist in the West until the modern era. Admittedly all three institutions are based on human impulses and aspirations that are universal. But these aspirations were given a unique expression in Western civilization, largely due to the influence of Athens and Jerusalem—Athens representing the principle of autonomous reason and Jerusalem representing the revealed truths of Judaism and Christianity.

First let us consider science. It is based on a shared human trait: the desire to know. People in every culture have tried to learn about the world. Thus the Chinese recorded the eclipses, the Mayans developed a calendar, the Hindus discovered the number zero, and so on. But science—which requires experiments, and laboratories, and induction, and verification, and what one scholar has termed "the invention of invention"—is a Western institution. This explains why the vast majority of major inventions in the past few hundred years have occurred in the West. If science were not a Western institution, there would be no way to account for this disproportion; indeed, we would be forced to conclude that the rest of the world was incredibly stupid.

Why did science develop in the West? This is a hugely complicated question and not one that I can fully answer. The best that I can do is to suggest two lines of thought that led the West in this direction. To locate the first, one has to go back to the ancient Greek philosophers. The ancient Greeks invented philosophy, which was an attempt to learn the truth about the world through unassisted human reason. No other ancient society placed so much confidence in reason. Philosophy as the Greeks understood it *included* science; it was a study of nature and of human nature. Greek philosophy from the time of Socrates emphasized the latter and thus made little headway in figuring out the mysteries of nature.

But even so, the Greeks came up with the notion that the universe as a whole makes sense, that it operates in accordance with laws, that these laws are accessible in principle to human reason, and that they can be expressed in the language of mathematics. It is important to realize that there is no logical reason why these things should be true. The influential Muslim writer al-Ghazali denies them. In *The Incoherence of Philosophy,* he argues that reason and logic are useless in apprehending the universe because Allah intervenes at every single moment to make things happen in the way that they do. This represented the Muslim version of the belief in an "enchanted universe" governed by spirits that is characteristic of many ancient peoples. To believe in the Greek notion of a reality that is not arbitrary, that obeys mathematical laws, a reality that is reasonable and susceptible to human understanding, is to have a certain kind of faith—a faith in reason.

The Greeks did, and in subsequent centuries this faith was strengthened in the West by the Christian notion of a divine being who embodies reason and truth and who created the universe and man.[20] Many of the greatest scientists of the West—among them, Copernicus, Kepler, Boyle, and Newton—believed that their work demonstrated the hidden hand of God in the universe. Their science was inspired and fortified by their Christian faith. The faith is much weaker among scientists today; probably very few practicing scientists see their work as confirming a divine presence. But all of them, even those who have never heard of the Greeks and who reject Christianity, nevertheless operate on the Greek and Christian assumption that reality is rational. Without this assumption, without this faith, science itself becomes impossible.

A second notion that is crucial to the development of science is the idea of development itself—the idea of progress. Sociologist Robert Nisbet terms it "one of the master ideas of the West."[21]

We see it, for instance, in the teenager who says to her mother, "Mom, how can you believe that? This is 2002!" That cliché is freighted with philosophical significance: it presumes a higher consciousness for the present than existed in the past. The belief in progress is also evident in the widespread expectation that our knowledge and our economy will continue to grow, and that our children will know more and have a better life than we do. Europeans and American take these things for granted, but they are novel concepts that arose quite recently in the West.

The idea of progress, like the idea of reason, is a doctrine that cannot be proved but must be taken on faith. The Greeks didn't have this faith: they believed that history moves in cycles. One may say that the Greeks believed in change, but not in progress. To the degree that the Greeks found a pattern in this change, it was largely one of degeneration. For many Greek thinkers, the golden age was in the past and things had been going steadily downhill since then. Of course the Greeks admitted that things could get better, but they believed that they could just as easily get worse. What governed human destiny was chance or fate. These notions of cyclical change and degeneration and fate were not unique to the Greeks. They were shared by the Hindus, the Muslims, the Buddhists, the Confucian Chinese, and by virtually everyone else in the world.

The modern West is the only civilization to entertain the idea that there is a meaningful pattern in history, that this pattern is onward and upward, that knowledge is cumulative and that its applications to human betterment are continuous and never-ending, that the future is certain to be better than the past. "Utopia" is in this sense a Western concept, because it locates perfection in the future. For most people in the world these notions—that history is somehow encoded with meaning, that we know in advance that things will improve instead of degenerate—are even today considered nothing short of ridiculous. In the West, too, the idea of progress continues to be debated. For instance, there is ongoing argument about whether progress is comprehensive, i.e., whether progress involves only material gains or also moral gains. But in some form the faith in progress is very widespread in the West, and the belief in it holds because it is supported by the contemporary experience of the people of the West.

Where, then, did the Western belief in progress come from? From Christianity. It is Christianity that introduced the idea of a divine plan for man and the world. In this view, history was not one meaningless event after another: it represented the fulfillment of a story line—a story line that began with the Fall but would end in triumph with the Second Coming of Christ. The Christian narrative is one of Creation, Incarnation, and Last Judgment. As J. B. Bury points out in *The Idea of Progress,* the Christian doctrine by itself does not generate the notion of progress; for this to happen it must be secularized.[22] This is done by keeping the concept of development but introducing man as its author and instrument. Human beings, building upon the discoveries of the past and of each other, will assure the continual advance of knowledge and its application to the betterment of the human condition. This is the idea that we recognize as "progress." The idea of progress is a secular expression of the idea of providence.

I think I have given some indication of why science is a Western institution, and of how it developed in the West. Now let me suggest why democracy and capitalism, too, are Western. Democracy is based on a broad human aspiration: the aspiration to be heard and to participate in decision-making. Other cultures have accommodated this aspiration: we can imagine a village leader, in Asia or Africa, soliciting input from his people as he makes an important decision. Tribal participation in this sense is universal. But democracy—by which I mean free elections, and peaceful transitions of power, and representative government, and separation of powers, and checks and balances—is a Western idea. The ancient Greeks had a version of democracy. Theirs was direct rather than representative democracy—the people made decisions themselves, rather than electing others to do so on their behalf. Moreover, Greek democracy was a kind of aristocracy because it excluded slaves, women, and resident aliens, and thus limited the franchise to a very small percentage of the population. It is the modern West that first invented the notion of representative democracy based on an expansion of the franchise and on the consent of the governed.

Capitalism, too, is based on a universal human impulse—the impulse to barter and trade. All societies have engaged in some form of exchange. Even the use of money is not Western in origin. But capitalism—by which I mean property rights, and contracts, and courts to enforce them, and free trade; in short, the whole ensemble of arrangements that Adam Smith described in *The Wealth of Nations*—is a Western institution. Modern capitalism also requires limited-liability corporations, stock exchanges, patents, insurance, double-entry bookkeeping, and legal limits on state seizure of assets. This framework also developed in the West.

Moreover, there is the psychology that is critical to capitalist success. Capitalism is based on the belief that the calling of the merchant or entrepreneur is a worthwhile one. In most societies merchants and entrepreneurs have been regarded as lowlife scum, and for centuries this prejudice was also held in the West. How this prejudice was overcome is a story that I must reserve for the next chapter.

Here I am content to argue that it is the interaction between the three Western institutions of science, democracy, and capitalism that has produced the great wealth and strength and success of Western civilization. An example of this interaction: one of the most powerful engines of that success, technology, arises out of the marriage between science and capitalism. Science provides the knowledge that leads to invention, and capitalism supplies the mechanism by which the invention is transmitted to the larger society, as well as the economic incentive for inventors to continue to make new things.

Now we can understand better why the West was able, between the sixteenth century and the nineteenth century, to subdue the rest of the world and bend it to its will. Indian elephants and Zulu spears were no match for British jeeps and rifles. Colonialism and imperialism are not the *cause* of the West's success; they are the *result* of that success. The wealth and military power of the European nations made them arrogant and stimulated their appetite for global conquest: thus the British, the Dutch, and the French went abroad in search of countries to subdue and rule. These colonial possessions added to the prestige, and to a lesser degree to the wealth, of Europe. But the primary cause of Western affluence and power is internal—the institutions of science, democracy, and capitalism acting in concert. Consequently it is simply wrong to maintain that the rest of the world is poor because the West is rich, or that the West grew rich off "stolen goods" from Asia, Africa, and Latin America, because the West created its own wealth, and still does. The doctrine of oppression ignores this fact, and continues to fuel anti-Western resentment around the world and within the nations of the West. I think we can now conclude that the doctrine is false, and the animus that is based on it is misplaced.

CHAPTER THREE

BECOMING AMERICAN
Why the American Idea Is Unique

The idea of right is simply that of
virtue introduced into the political world.

—ALEXIS DE TOCQUEVILLE

A HUNDRED YEARS AGO, WESTERN CIVILIZATION ENJOYED unchallenged political and military supremacy, but its domination of the world was incomplete, even fragile. The reason for this is given in Milton's line from *Paradise Lost*, "Who overcomes by force hath overcome but half his foe." Even if some aspects of Western civilization were welcomed by the native peoples of Asia, Africa, and Latin America, by and large Western domination was the product of conquest and military superiority. The British, for example, governed India with the police power of 100,000 troops. The rulers were able to secure the conformity, but not the support, of the native peoples. Eventually native leaders emerged who resolved to fight, and uproot, European rule from their soil. The Europeans saw this happening, and therefore the mood at the dawn of the twentieth century was somber. Intelligent Europeans knew that there was a good chance that the whole colonial enterprise might fall apart.

So it did. The twentieth century witnessed the rise of liberation movements throughout Asia, Africa, and South America in resistance to colonialism and Western domination. Within the West, civil rights movements led by black and brown people demanded the extension of full citizenship and equal rights to minorities that had previously been excluded and discriminated against. These movements met with resistance, political as well as military. In some places, the natives fought guerrilla wars against the colonial powers. But ultimately the nonwhite peoples of the world prevailed. They did not secure their freedom by inflicting a military defeat on the West. This they did not have the power to do. They won by appealing to the principles of the West, including the principle of self-determination, and by shaming the West into relinquishing its empire and granting independence to its former colonies.

One of my high-school teachers in India liked to say, "If Hitler had been ruling India, Gandhi would be a lamp shade." This man was not known for his sensitivity, but he had a habit of speaking the truth. His point was that the success of Gandhi and of the Indian protesters, who prostrated themselves on the train tracks, depended on the certain knowledge that the trains would stop rather than run over them. With tactics such as these, Gandhi and his followers hoped to paralyze British rule in India, and they succeeded. But what if the British had ordered the trains to keep going? This is certainly what Hitler would have done. I don't see Genghis Khan or Attila the Hun being deterred by Gandhi's strategy. Even as the Indians denounced the West as wholly unprincipled and immoral, they relied on Western principles and Western morality to secure their independence.

One by one the nations of South America, Asia, and Africa won their freedom. Indeed, anticolonialism was the dominant political trajectory of much of the twentieth century. By the middle of the century, so rapid was the momentum of anticolonialism that it seemed to imperil the confidence, perhaps even the identity, of Western civilization. A deep pessimism descended on many in the West. The mood is conveyed by James Burnham's *Suicide of the West*, published in 1964. Burnham began his book by noting that, in 1914, nearly the whole world fell under the domain of the West. Now, he said, the West has lost virtually all its colonial possessions. Moreover, Burnham fretted, the Soviet Union has become a world power and has conquered all of Eastern Europe, in the very heart of Western civilization. These are stunning losses for the West, Burnham said, and since history shows that defeats of this magnitude are seldom reversed, "It is probable that the West, in shrinking, is also dying." At the current rate of dissolution, Burnham concluded, in a few decades "the West will be finished."[1]

Oddly enough, some leading thinkers in the West argued that the decline and even destruction of the West was a good thing. These figures can be seen as the forerunners of today's multiculturalists; for them, a defeat for the West inevitably counted as a gain for humanity. "Europe is at death's door," exulted philosopher Jean Paul Sartre. "Europe is springing leaks everywhere. In the past we made history and now it is being made of us. The ratio of forces has been inverted; decolonization has begun."[2]

As Burnham and Sartre recognized, many of the newly free nations defined themselves in opposition to the West. Some allied themselves openly with the Soviet Union. Others, seeking a "third way" that eschewed both Soviet communism and Western capitalism, assembled in 1955 at the Bandung Conference, where they proclaimed themselves Non-Aligned Nations. From the outset the rhetoric of nonalignment was a bit of a sham. Despite the posture of neutrality, the policies of most of these "nonaligned" nations, such as India and Cuba, were in practice pro-socialist and anti-Western. An objective observer who witnessed these developments would be justified in concluding that the prospects for the West were bleak.

Then, at the end of the century, a surprise! In 1989 the Berlin Wall came crashing down, and soon Eastern Europe was free. Eventually the Soviet Union itself imploded, and with the end of the Cold War the United States found itself the only remaining superpower. The West was back in the saddle, but this time it wasn't Europe but a former English colony, the United States, that was the dominant nation. America's power had been awesomely displayed as early as World War II, but not until the early 1990s did America begin to enjoy an unrivaled supremacy over the globe that was unprecedented in history.

Previous empires have controlled only regions of the world. The Roman Empire, the Islamic empire, and the British Empire, each had an awesome reach, but they left out large parts of humanity. American hegemony is unique in that it extends virtually over the total space of the inhabited earth. Also, previous empires have dominated their subjects through force. Once again America is different in that its influence is not primarily sustained by force. This is not to say that America never projects its military power abroad. But these projections of power cannot possibly explain the enormous appeal of the American idea around the globe.

Drop in at a hotel in Buenos Aires or Bombay, and the bellhop is whistling the theme song from *Titanic*. Take a train through a village in Africa or the Middle East, and you will see a young boy, seemingly untouched by Western civilization. When you look closer, however, you see that he is wearing an Orioles baseball cap. Moreover, he has the cap worn back-to-front, to show the adjusto-strap to advantage. The boy also has a sauntering walk that seems uncharacteristic and vaguely familiar. Then it hits you: The little fellow wants to be Chris Rock! He wants to be an American! I don't just mean that he wants American technology; everyone has wanted that for a long time. (Even the terrorists who proclaim "Death to America" like American technology.) Nor do I mean that he wants Western institutions, such as democracy or freedom of speech. No, he wants more than that: He wants the American way of life. He wants to "become an American."

Now that's superiority. This is not to suggest that the boy in the example is typical of boys his age, or that everybody in the world wants to put on a baseball cap. But it dramatizes the way in which many people are magnetically attracted to what America represents, whether it is American restaurants or Levi's jeans or Madonna or Mike Tyson or MTV. In China, we read, teenagers are adopting American styles and one of them tells *Forbes* that her American attire will make her "the coolest person in China."[3] India's prime minister, Atal Behari Vajpayee, recently confessed that his favorite movie is *The Lion King*.[4] In the Middle East,

American dolls have become so popular that an official of the Arab League frets that Barbie—with her miniskirts and career aspirations—is not a suitable role model for Muslim children.[5] Even in the Iranian holy city of Qom, right down the street from the mosque, the vendors are selling American CDs and videos.[6] Some Americans will scoff at these American exports, regarding them as foolish, trivial, or vulgar, but even if they are all those things, their universal appeal still has to be explained.

The advocates of multiculturalism seem chronically unable to do this. The ideologues who proclaim the equality of all cultures simply cannot account for why so many people around the world seem perfectly willing to dump their ancient cultures and adopt new ways of thinking, feeling, and acting that they associate with America. Nor can they account for the millions of people who have come as immigrants in search of the American dream. If all cultures are equal, why aren't people breaking down doors to get into Cuba or Iraq or Somalia?

All sensible people know the answer: those are terrible places to live. A much tougher question is what explains the enormous appeal of the United States to immigrants and to people around the world? This is a hard question because, as we will see, the obvious answers do not prove satisfactory. Moreover, there are lots of people who detest America. Bin Laden and his friends were willing to kill people from many countries but their specific target wasn't "Western civilization": it was the United States. The enemies of America—and what it stands for—don't all live abroad; quite a few are American citizens. And some of the local critics are no less venomous than their foreign counterparts. So any explanation of the appeal of America must also account for this resistance. Why is the American idea simultaneously attractive and yet controversial?

Critics of America, both at home and abroad, have an easy explanation for why the American idea is so captivating, and why immigrants want to come here. The reason, they say, is money. America represents "the bitch goddess of success." That is why poor people reach out for the American idea: they want to touch some of that lucre. As for immigrants, they allegedly flock to the United States for the sole purpose of getting rich. This view, which represents the appeal of America as the appeal of the almighty dollar, is disseminated on Arab streets and in multicultural textbooks taught in U.S. schools. It is a way of demeaning the United States by associating it with what is selfish, base, and crass: an unquenchable appetite for gain.

It is not hard to see why this view of America has gained a wide currency. When people in foreign countries turn on American TV shows, they are stupefied by the lavish displays of affluence: the sumptuous homes, the bejeweled women, the fountains and pools, and so on. Whether reruns of *Dallas* and *Dynasty* are true to the American experience is irrelevant here; the point is that this is how the United States appears to outsiders who have not had the chance to come here. And even for those who do, it is hard to deny that America represents the chance to live better, even to become fantastically wealthy. For instance, there are several people of Indian descent on the *Forbes* 400 list. And over the years I have heard many Indians now living in the United States say, "We want to live an Indian lifestyle, but at an American standard of living."

If this seems like a crass motive for immigration, it must be evaluated in the context of the harsh fate that poor people endure in much of the Third World. The lives of many of these people are defined by an ongoing struggle to exist. It is not that they don't work hard. On the contrary, they labor incessantly and endure hardships that are almost unimaginable to people in the West. In the villages of Asia and Africa, for example, a common sight is a farmer beating a pickax into the ground, women wobbling under heavy loads, children carrying stones. These people are performing very hard labor, but they are getting nowhere. The best they can hope for is to survive for another day. Their clothes are tattered, their teeth are rotted, and disease and death constantly loom over their horizon. For the poor of the Third World, life is characterized by squalor, indignity, and brevity.

I emphasize the plight of the poor, but I recognize, of course, that there are substantial middle classes even in the underdeveloped world. For these people basic survival may not be an issue, but still, they endure hardships that make everyday life a strain. One problem is that the basic infrastructure of the Third World is abysmal: the roads are not properly paved, the water is not safe to drink, pollution in the cities has reached hazardous levels, public transportation is overcrowded and unreliable, and there is a two-year waiting period to get a telephone. Government officials, who are very poorly paid, are inevitably corrupt, which means that you must pay bribes on a regular basis to get things done. Most important, there are limited prospects for the children's future.

In America, the immigrant immediately recognizes, things are different. The newcomer who sees America for the first time typically experiences emotions that alternate between wonder and delight. Here is a country where *everything works*: the roads are clean and paper smooth, the highway signs are clear and accurate, the public toilets function properly, when you pick up the telephone you get a dial tone, you can even buy things from the store and then take them back. For the Third World visitor, the American supermarket is a thing to behold: endless aisles of every imaginable product, fifty different types of cereal, multiple flavors of ice cream. The place is full of countless unappreciated inventions: quilted toilet paper, fabric softener, cordless telephones, disposable diapers, roll-on luggage, deodorant. Most countries even today do not have these benefits: deodorant, for example, is unavailable in much of the Third World and unused in much of Europe.

What the immigrant cannot help noticing is that America is a country where the poor live comparatively well. This fact was dramatized in the 1980s, when CBS television broadcast an anti-Reagan documentary, "People Like Us," which was intended to show the miseries of the poor during an American recession. The Soviet Union also broadcast the documentary, with a view to embarrassing the Reagan administration. But by the testimony of former Soviet leaders, it had the opposite effect. Ordinary people across the Soviet Union saw that the poorest Americans have television sets and microwave ovens and cars. They arrived at the same perception of America that I witnessed in a friend of mine from Bombay who has been unsuccessfully trying to move to the United States for nearly a decade. Finally I asked him, "Why are you so eager to come to America?" He replied, "Because I really want to live in a country where the poor people are fat."

The point is that the United States is a country where the ordinary guy has a good life. This is what distinguishes America from so many other countries. Everywhere in the world, the rich person lives well. Indeed, a good case can be made that if you are rich, you live better in countries other than America. The reason is that you enjoy the pleasures of aristocracy. This is the pleasure of being treated as a superior person. Its gratification derives from subservience: in India, for example, the wealthy enjoy the satisfaction of seeing innumerable servants and toadies grovel before them and attend to their every need.

In the United States the social ethic is egalitarian, and this is unaffected by the inequalities of wealth in the country. Tocqueville noticed this egalitarianism a century and a half ago, but it is, if anything, more prevalent today. For all his riches, Bill Gates could not approach a homeless person and say, "Here's a $100 bill. I'll give it to you if you kiss my feet." Most likely the homeless guy would tell Gates to go to hell! The American view is that the rich guy may have more money, but he isn't in any fundamental sense better than you are. The American janitor or waiter sees himself as performing a service, but he doesn't see himself as inferior to those he serves. And neither do the customers see him that way: they are generally happy to show him respect and appreciation on a plane of equality. America is the only country in the world where we call the waiter "Sir," as if he were a knight.

The moral triumph of America is that it has extended the benefits of comfort and affluence, traditionally enjoyed by very few, to a large segment of society. Very few people in America have to wonder where their next meal is coming from. Even sick people who don't have proper insurance can receive medical care at hospital emergency rooms. The poorest American girls are not humiliated by having to wear torn clothes. Every child is given an education, and most have the chance to go on to college. The common man can expect to live long enough and have free time to play with his grandchildren.

Ordinary Americans enjoy not only security and dignity, but also comforts that other societies reserve for the elite. We now live in a country where construction workers regularly pay $4 for a nonfat latte, where maids drive very nice cars, where plumbers take their families on vacation to Europe. As Irving Kristol once observed, there is virtually no restaurant in America to which a CEO can go to lunch with the absolute assurance that he will not find his secretary also dining there. Given the standard of living of the ordinary American, it is no wonder that socialist or revolutionary schemes have never found a wide constituency in the United States. As sociologist Werner Sombart observed, all socialist utopias in America have come to grief on roast beef and apple pie.[7]

Thus it is entirely understandable that people would associate the idea of America with a better life. For them, money is not an end in itself; money is the means to a longer, healthier, and fuller life. Money allows them to purchase a level of security, dignity, and comfort that they could not have hoped to enjoy in their native countries. Money also frees up time for family life, community involvement, and spiritual pursuits: thus it produces not just material, but also moral, gains. All of this is true, and yet in my view it offers an incomplete picture of why America is so appealing to so many. Let me illustrate with the example of my own life.

Not long ago, I asked myself: what would my life have been like if I had never come to the United States, if I had stayed in India? Materially, my life has improved, but not in a fundamental sense. I grew up in a middle-class family in Bombay. My father was a chemical engineer; my mother, an office secretary. I was raised without great luxury, but neither did I lack for anything. My standard of living in America is higher, but it is not a radical difference. My life has changed far more dramatically in other ways.

If I had remained in India, I would probably have lived my entire existence within a one-mile radius of where I was born. I would undoubtedly have married a woman of my identical religious, socioeconomic, and cultural background. I would almost certainly have become a medical doctor, an engineer, or a software programmer. I would have socialized within my ethnic community and had cordial relations, but few friends, outside that group. I would have a whole set of opinions that could be predicted in advance; indeed, they would not be very different from what my father believed, or his father before him. In sum, my destiny would to a large degree have been given to me.

This is not to say that I would have no choice; I would have choice, but within narrowly confined parameters. Let me illustrate with the example of my sister, who got married several years ago. My parents began the process by conducting a comprehensive survey of all the eligible families in our neighborhood. First they examined primary criteria, such as religion, socioeconomic position, and educational background. Then my parents investigated subtler issues: the social reputation of the family, reports of a lunatic uncle, the character of the son, and so on. Finally my parents were down to a dozen or so eligible families, and they were invited to our house for dinner with suspicious regularity. My sister was, in the words of Milton Friedman, "free to choose." My sister knew about, and accepted, the arrangement; she is now happily married with two children. I am not quarreling with the outcome, but clearly my sister's destiny was, to a considerable extent, choreographed by my parents.

By coming to America, I have seen my life break free of these traditional confines. I came to Arizona as an exchange student, but a year later I was enrolled at Dartmouth College. There I fell in with a group of students who were actively involved in politics; soon I had switched my major from economics to English literature. My reading included books like Plutarch's *Moralia*; Hamilton, Madison, and Jay's *Federalist Papers*; and Evelyn Waugh's *Brideshead Revisited*. They transported me to places a long way from home and implanted in my mind ideas that I had never previously considered. By the time I graduated, I decided that I should become a writer, which is something you can do in this country. America permits many strange careers: this is a place where you can become, say, a comedian. I would not like to go to my father and tell him that I was thinking of becoming a comedian. I do not think he would have found it funny.

Soon after graduation I became the managing editor of a policy magazine and began to write freelance articles in the *Washington Post*. Someone in the Reagan White House was apparently impressed by my work, because I was called in for an interview and promptly hired as a senior domestic policy analyst. I found it strange to be working at the White House, because at the time I was not a United States citizen. I am sure that such a thing would not happen in India or anywhere else in the world. But Reagan and his people didn't seem to mind; for them, ideology counted more than nationality. I also met my future wife in the Reagan administration, where she was at the time a White House intern. (She has since deleted it from her résumé.) My wife was born in Louisiana and grew up in San Diego; her ancestry is English, French, Scotch-Irish, German, and American Indian.

I notice that Americans marry in a rather peculiar way: by falling in love. You may think that I am being ironic, or putting you on, so let me hasten to inform you that in many parts of the world, romantic love is considered a mild form of insanity. Consider a typical situation: Anjali is in love with Arjun. She considers Arjun the best-looking man in the world, the most intelligent, virtually without fault, a paragon of humanity! But everybody else can see that Arjun is none of these things. What, then, persuades Anjali that Arjun possesses qualities that are nowhere in evidence? There is only one explanation: Anjali is deeply deluded. It does not follow that her romantic impulses should be ruthlessly crushed. But, in the view of many people and many traditions around the world, they should be steered and directed and prevented from ruining Anjali's life. This is the job of parents and the community, to help Anjali see beyond her delusions and to make decisions that are based on practical considerations and common sense.

If there is a single phrase that encapsulates life in the Third World, it is that "birth is destiny." I remember an incident years ago when my grandfather called in my brother, my sister, and me, and asked us if we knew how lucky we were. We asked him why he felt this way: was it because we were intelligent, or had lots of friends, or were blessed with a loving family? Each time he shook his head and said, "No." Finally we pressed him: why did he consider us so lucky? Then he revealed the answer: "Because you are Brahmins!"

The Brahmin, who is the highest ranking in the Hindu caste system, is traditionally a member of the priestly class. As a matter of fact, my family had nothing to do with the priesthood. Nor are we Hindu: my ancestors converted to Christianity many generations ago. Even so, my grandfather's point was that before we converted, hundreds of years ago, our family used to be Brahmins. How he knew this remains a mystery. But he was serious in his insistence that nothing that the three of us achieved in life could possibly mean more than the fact that we were Brahmins.

This may seem like an extreme example, revealing my grandfather to be a very narrow fellow indeed, but the broader point is that traditional cultures attach a great deal of importance to data such as what tribe you come from, whether you are male or female, and whether you are the eldest son. Your destiny and your happiness hinge on these things. If you are a Bengali, you can count on other Bengalis to help you, and on others to discriminate against you; if you are female, then certain forms of society and several professions are closed to you; and if you are the eldest son, you inherit the family house and your siblings are expected to follow your direction. What this means is that once your tribe, caste, sex, and family position have been established at birth, your life takes a course that is largely determined for you.

In America, by contrast, you get to write the script of your own life. When your parents say to you, "What do you want to be when you grow up?" the question is open-ended; it is you who supply the answer. Your parents can advise you: "Have you considered law school?" "Why not become the first doctor in the family?" It is considered very improper, however, for them to try and force your decision. Indeed, American parents typically send their teenage children away to college, where they live on their own and learn independence. This is part of the process of forming your mind and choosing a field of interest for yourself and developing your identity. It is not uncommon in the United States for two brothers who come from the same gene pool and were raised in similar circumstances to do quite different things: the eldest becomes a gas station attendant, the younger moves up to be vice president at Oracle; the eldest marries his high-school sweetheart and raises four kids, the youngest refuses to settle down, or comes out of the closet as a homosexual; one is the Methodist that he was raised to be, the other becomes a Christian Scientist or a Buddhist. What to be, where to live, whom to love, whom to marry, what to believe, what religion to practice—these are all decisions that Americans make for themselves.

In most parts of the world your identity and your fate are to a large extent handed to you; in America, you determine them for yourself. In America your destiny is not prescribed; it is constructed. Your life is like a blank sheet of paper, and you are the artist. This notion of you being the architect of your own destiny is the incredibly powerful idea that is behind the worldwide appeal of America. Young people especially find irresistible the prospect of being in the driver's seat, of authoring the narrative of their own lives. So too the immigrant discovers that America permits him to break free of the constraints that have held him captive, so that the future becomes a landscape of his own choosing.

The phrase that captures this unique aspect of America is the "pursuit of happiness." Nobel laureate V. S. Naipaul analyzes the concept in this way: "It is an elastic idea; it fits all men. It implies a certain kind of society, a certain kind of awakened spirit. So much is contained in it: the idea of the individual, responsibility, choice, the life of the intellect, the idea of vocation and perfectibility and achievement. It is an immense human idea. It cannot be reduced to a fixed system. It cannot generate fanaticism. But it is known to exist; and because of that, other more rigid systems in the end blow away."[8]

☆☆☆

But where did the "pursuit of happiness" come from? How did America develop a unique framework for enabling people to shape their own destiny? I have been speaking autobiographically, so let me put the question in a more general way. Consider New York City. It is a tumultuous place, teeming with diversity: Wall Street hustlers, struggling artists, Pakistani cabdrivers, female book editors, philosophically-minded barbers, elderly women walking dogs, "Big Tony" with the hairy armpits serving pizza, and eccentrics of every stripe. New York has black and white, rich and poor, immigrant and native. I notice two striking things about these people. They are energetic, hardworking, opportunistic: they want to succeed, and believe there is a good chance they can. Second, for all their profound differences, they all manage somehow to get along. This raises a question about New York, and about America: how does it manage to reconcile such fantastic ethnic and religious and socioeconomic diversity and give hope and inspiration to so many people from all over the world?

I intend to answer this question, but first I want to mention a darker side of New York and America that has not escaped the attention of their critics. To the Islamic fundamentalist, the most striking aspect about New York is not its wealth or its diversity but its debauchery. From the point of view of many Muslims, and of some American conservatives too, New York City is Sin City. There debauchery not only seems prevalent, but even worse, it seems socially accepted.

This raises Sayyid Qutb's argument that America may be a peaceful and a prosperous society but it is fundamentally an immoral society. Qutb would not be impressed by New York's great productivity or its varied cuisine or the fact that people of different backgrounds get along together. He would dismiss all that as worthless triviality. He makes his argument on the highest level. In the good society, he contends, it is God, and not man, who rules. God is the source of all authority, including legitimate political authority. Virtue, not freedom, is the highest value. Therefore God's commands, not man's laws, should govern the society. The goal of the regime is to make people better, not to make them better off.

Qutb's theocratic argument falls harshly on American ears, but let us recall that it is substantially the argument made by Plato and the classical philosophers, who argued that the best regime is devoted to inculcating virtue. Plato's argument is that the ideal arrangement for a society is to have the wise people as rulers. No one can be against this, especially in view of the alternative, which is rule of the stupid or unwise. In Plato's view, the wisest people are necessarily a small minority; in particular, they are the philosophers. Plato's argument against democracy is that it mistakes quantity for quality: it prefers the choices of the uninformed multitude to those who really know what they are doing. In Plato's view, democracy is the rule of unwise people by unwise people.

In theory, we have to concede that Plato and Qutb are right. Every society should seek to be ruled by its best people, and, to take the point further, who would make a better and more just ruler than an omniscient God? Moreover, it would be silly to insist that God issue a set of laws or rules; better to let Him use divine discretion and decide each case on its merits. Nor is there any question of God submitting to election or popular referendum: why should divine wisdom, which is infallible, be subject to the consent of the unwise?

But let us not be hasty in trying to implement these schemes. Even as we concede, in principle, the validity of the doctrine articulated in Plato's *Republic*, it cannot escape our notice that he has not given us a portrait of an actual city. Rather, his is a "city in speech," a utopia; even Plato does not expect to see it realized. There are, of course, Islamic theocracies. The Taliban had one in Afghanistan, and several other Muslim countries, notably Iran, operate on the premise that they are being ruled by Allah's decrees. But far from being replicas of paradise on earth, these places seem to be characterized by widespread misery, discontent, tyranny, and inequality. Is God, then, such an incompetent ruler?

In reality, Iran is not ruled by God; it is ruled by politicians and mullahs who claim to act on God's behalf. Right away we see the two problems with Qutb's doctrine. First, Allah's teaching must be divined or interpreted by man, and this raises the question of whether the revelation is authentic and the interpretation accurate. Second, people inevitably disagree over what Allah is saying, or about how his edict applies in a given situation, so inevitably there must be some human means of adjudicating the conflict. In some cases people may even reject Allah himself, preferring the wisdom of the Christian God or that of their own minds. What is to be done with them?

Islam has solutions to these problems, and they are stern ones. Through an elaborate system of Koranic law, precedent, and tradition, Islamic societies seek to apply divine wisdom to a multitude of situations. Since no law, however detailed, can anticipate every human circumstance, in practice this approach places divine authority at the discretion of mullahs and other authorities, who can use it to have people fined, jailed, flogged, dismembered, or killed. Such sentences are quite common in Islamic societies. As for dissenters and nonbelievers, Islamic societies have traditionally dealt with them with predictable severity. Islamic rulers required Christians and Jews to pay a special tax and to agree to a whole set of religious and social restrictions (no proselytizing, no bearing arms, restrictions on intermarriage, bans on taking certain government posts, no testifying against a Muslim in court, and so on) that effectively made them second-class citizens. As for atheists, polytheists, and apostates, Islamic rulers gave them a simple choice: accept Allah or be killed.[9]

Before we wax too indignant about Islam's intolerance, let us remember that Christianity traditionally was even more intolerant. Medieval Christians generally had no compunction about expelling Jews, burning heretics, and obtaining confessions with the sword. Muslim rulers may have forced Christians and Jews to be second-class citizens, but some Christian rulers refused to permit Muslims and Jews to be citizens at all. And when Christianity split into Catholic and Protestant, the two camps set upon each other with a sanguinary vengeance. The American founders were all too familiar with the history of the religious wars, which wreaked havoc and destruction in Europe, and they were determined to avoid that bloodshed here.

The founders who confronted the problem of religion were themselves religious men—not orthodox Christians, but Deists—who would have agreed with Qutb that political legitimacy derives from God. I realize that this view runs counter to what many Americans are taught: that America's system of government emerged in resistance to the doctrine of the divine right of kings. Yet the Declaration of Independence clearly states that the source of our rights is "our Creator." It is because our rights come from God, and not from ourselves, that they are "unalienable." Thus we see that America, too, was founded on divine right: the only difference is that sovereignty is transferred from the one (the king) to the many (the people).

Despite the religious foundation for the American system of government, the founders were determined not to permit theological differences to become the basis for political conflict. The solution they came up with was as simple as it was unique: separation of religion and government. This is not the same thing as religious tolerance. Think about what tolerance means. If I *tolerate* you, that implies I believe you are *wrong*, I *object* to your views, but I will *put up* with you. (If I found your views congenial, there would be no question of tolerance.) In line with this thinking, England had enacted a series of acts of religious toleration. But England also had an official church. The American system went beyond toleration in refusing to establish a national church and in recognizing that all citizens were free to practice their religion.

One reason that separation of religion and government worked is that from the beginning the United States was made up of numerous, mostly Protestant, sects. The Puritans dominated in Massachusetts, the Anglicans in Virginia, the Catholics were concentrated in Maryland, and so on. No group was strong enough to subdue all the others, and so it was in every group's interest to "live and let live." The ingenuity of the American solution is evident in Voltaire's remark that where there is one religion, you have tyranny; where there are two, you have religious war; but where there are many, you have freedom.[10]

A second reason the American founders were able to avoid religious oppression and conflict is that they found a way to channel people's energies away from theological quarrels and into commercial activity. The American system is founded on property rights and trade, and *The Federalist* tells us that the protection of the unequal faculties of obtaining property is "the first object of government."[11] The logic of this position is best expressed by Samuel Johnson's remark, "There are few ways in which a man is so innocently occupied than in getting money."[12] The founders reasoned that people who are working assiduously to better their condition, people who are planning to make an addition to their kitchen, and who are saving up for a vacation, are not likely to go around spearing their neighbors.

Capitalism gives America a this-worldly focus, in which death and the afterlife recede from everyday view. (This is why funerals are an uncommon and distressing sight in America.) The gaze of the people is shifted from heavenly aspirations to earthly progress. This "lowering of the sights" convinces many critics that American capitalism is a base, degraded system and the energies that drive it are crass and immoral. These modern critiques draw on some very old prejudices. In the ancient world, labor was generally despised and in some cases even ambition was seen as reprehensible. Think about the lines from *Julius Caesar*, "The noble Brutus hath told you Caesar was ambitious." And here you might expect Mark Antony to say, "And what's wrong with that?" But he goes on, "If it were so, it was a grievous fault."[13]

In all the cultures of antiquity, Western as well as non-Western, the merchant and the trader were viewed as lowlife scum. The Greeks looked down on their merchants, and the Spartans tried to stamp out the profession altogether. "The gentleman understands what is noble," Confucius writes in his *Analects*. "The small man understands what is profitable."[14] In the Indian caste system the *vaisya* or trader occupies nearly the lowest rung of the ladder—one step up from the despised untouchable. The Muslim historian Ibn Khaldun suggests that even gain by conquest is preferable to gain by trade, because conquest embodies the virtues of courage and manliness.[15] In these traditions, the honorable life is devoted to philosophy or the priesthood or military valor. "Making a living" was considered a necessary, but undignified, pursuit. As Ibn Khaldun would have it, far better to rout your adversary, kill the men, enslave the women and children, and make off with a bunch of loot than to improve your lot by buying and selling stuff.

Drawing on the inspiration of modern philosophers like Locke and Adam Smith, the American founders altered this moral hierarchy. They argued that trade based on consent and mutual gain was preferable to plunder. The founders established a regime in which the self-interest of entrepreneurs and workers would be directed toward serving the wants and needs of others. In this view, the ordinary life, devoted to production, serving the customer, and supporting a family, is a noble and dignified endeavor. Hard work, once considered a curse, now becomes socially acceptable, even honorable. Commerce, formerly a degraded thing, now becomes a virtue.

Of course the founders recognized that both in the private and the public sphere, greedy and ambitious people might pose a danger to the well-being of others. Instead of trying to outlaw these passions, the founders attempted a different approach. As the fifty-first book of *The Federalist* puts it, "Ambition must be made to counteract ambition." The argument is that in a free society "the security for civil rights must be the same as that for religious rights. It consists in the one case in the multiplicity of interests, in the other in the multiplicity of sects."[16] The framers of the Constitution reasoned that by setting interests against each other, by making them compete, no single one could become strong enough to imperil the welfare of the whole.

In the public sphere the founders took special care to devise a system that would prevent, or at least minimize, the abuse of power. To this end they established limited government, in order that the power of the state would remain confined. They divided authority between the national and state governments. Within the national framework, they provided for separation of powers, so that the legislature, executive, and judiciary would each have its own domain of power. They insisted upon checks and balances, to enhance accountability.

In general the founders adopted a "policy of supplying, by opposite and rival interests, the defect of better motives."[17] This is not to say that the founders ignored the importance of virtue. But they knew that virtue is not always in abundant supply. The Greek philosophers held that virtue was the same thing as knowledge—that people do bad things because they are ignorant—but the American founders did not agree. Their view was closer to that of St. Paul: "The good that I would, I do not. The evil that I would not, that I do."[18] According to Christianity, the problem of the bad person is that his will is corrupted, and this is a fault endemic to human nature. The American founders knew they could not transform human nature, so they devised a system that would thwart the schemes of the wicked and channel the energies of flawed persons toward the public good.

The experiment that the founders embarked upon two centuries ago has largely succeeded in achieving its goals. We see the evidence in New York, which presents an amazing sight to the world. Tribal and religious battles, such as we see in Lebanon, Mogadishu, Kashmir, and Belfast, don't happen here. In New York restaurants, white and African-American secretaries have lunch together. In Silicon Alley, Americans of Jewish and Palestinian descent collaborate on e-commerce solutions and play racquetball after work. Hindus and Muslims, Serbs and Croats, Turks and Armenians, Irish Catholics and British Protestants, all seem to have forgotten their ancestral differences and joined the vast and varied parade of New Yorkers. Everybody wants to "make it," to "get ahead," to "hit it big." And even as they compete, people recognize that somehow they are all in this together, in pursuit of some great, elusive American dream. In this respect New York is a resplendent symbol of America.

My conclusion is that the American founders solved two great problems—the problem of scarcity, and the problem of diversity—that were a source of perennial misery and conflict in ancient societies, and that remain unsolved in the regimes of contemporary Islam. The founders invented a new regime in which citizens would enjoy a wide berth of freedom—economic freedom, political freedom, and freedom of speech and religion—in order to shape their own lives and pursue happiness. By separating religion from government, and by directing the energies of the citizens toward trade and commerce, the American founders created a rich, dynamic, and tolerant society that is now the hope of countless immigrants and a magnet for the world.

Despite the fantastic scope and opportunity that America provides, many immigrants experience occasional ambivalence and anguish about their adopted country. My colleague Shelby Steele terms this "the shock of freedom." I see it more as the anxiety of displacement. In any event, immigrants commonly report feelings of uncertainty, loss, loneliness—a sense of being adrift in unfamiliar waters. To some extent these are the natural sentiments of one who is trying to find his way in a new society. What is new is that immigrants today encounter a multicultural ideology that encourages them to cling to their native ways, to resist assimilation, to "affirm their differences."

From the multicultural perspective, asking the immigrant to "become an American" is forcing him to give up who he is. In this view, assimilation is an expression of bigotry, because the non-white immigrant is required to put on a white cultural strait-jacket.[19] Multiculturalists say that white Americans should be the ones who adapt: they should learn to respect and cherish cultural differences. The multiculturalists regard the "melting pot" as a racist concept. In their view, immigrants should maintain their native identity and their traditional customs. The multiculturalists want immigrants to be in America but not of America.

But this does not seem to be what most immigrants want. The reason is simple: if the immigrant wanted to preserve intact his native culture, if he wanted to be the same person that he was in his home country, then why come to the United States? Clearly the immigrant seeks something that is available here and not in his homeland. That something, I have suggested, is the opportunity to have a good life, but more important, the chance to make his own life.

Most immigrants realize that this requires adapting to the cultural strategies of success in the United States. There is nothing bigoted or racist about this. It does not mean that, in order for me to become American, I have to quit playing the sitar and stop eating curry. I can preserve elements of my native culture and still wholeheartedly participate in the American way of life. This was not always the case with earlier generations of immigrants, who were pressured to abandon their old lives and become completely new people. A century ago, one social worker in New York noted of a family that had recently arrived from Sicily, "Not yet Americanized. Still eating Italian food."[20] The nativist prejudice was that "Italian-Americans" were somehow incomplete Americans.

As Teddy Roosevelt put it with characteristic pugnacity, "There is no room in this country for hyphenated Americans."[21]

But this is too harsh, and makes unnecessary and unreasonable demands on immigrants. A much better idea is the "melting pot," which emerged in *resistance* to the nativist doctrine. The melting pot concept is that immigrants bring something new and valuable to America, just as America has much that is new and valuable to offer them. So immigrants change America, and America changes the immigrants. Pizza and hamburgers, once alien imports from Italy and Germany, have become quintessentially American foods. Chinese food is now well established, and Indian and Thai dishes are also quite popular. While Americans benefit from this variety of cuisine, immigrants, too, realize that they have choices. In India I ate curry and rice every day; now I have the option of eating southern fried chicken or enchiladas. Why, then, should I hold onto my native culture and limit myself to the options my ancestors had?

I am using the example of cuisine to make the broader point that ethnicity in the Old World is involuntary, but in America it is, to a large degree, chosen. Think about it this way: Mario Cuomo's grandfather had no choice but to be Italian. That was an identity that was imposed on him. It defined who he was, what he ate, what he believed. But with the grandson it is a different story. No one is more Italian than Mario Cuomo—on Columbus Day. When he speaks before the Anti-Defamation League, however, he sings a different melody. I am quite sure Mario Cuomo likes pasta, but I doubt that it encompasses the whole of his cuisine. He has chosen what he wants to retain from the Old World and what he wants to relinquish. As an American, his Italian heritage is only one part of Mario Cuomo's identity.

I have been speaking of ethnicity largely in the cosmetic, super-ficial sense. At this surface level, it is possible for immigrants to live in several cultures. One doesn't have to choose between eating curry and eating southern fried chicken; one can do both. I can watch a Hindi film this week and Harrison Ford's latest thriller the next week. But at the deeper level, this is not possible. Cultures are fundamentally rooted in the *cult,* and they embody worldviews that are sometimes incompatible and irreconcilable. Either I consult my parents about whom to marry, or I decide for myself. Either I remain a Buddhist, or I become a Catholic, or give up my religion altogether. The point is that I cannot do all these things simultaneously; I have to choose.

Here is another example. In most Asian countries, the basic premise is that older people are wiser. Age is believed to confer the wisdom that derives from experience. This was the basis of ancestor worship in China; it helps to explain why, even today, the Chinese tend to be ruled by octogenarians. In America, however, the whole culture seems oriented around the preferences of fourteen-year-olds. Youth, not old age, sets the tone. There are reasons for these cultural differences, of course. Technology confers a decisive advantage on the young: they may not know about the Depression or World War II, but they do know how to program their VCRs and record messages on their answering machines. In a fast-changing, technological society, the young are "with it" and the old are constantly in danger of being "out of it."

My purpose here is not to say which way is better, but to say that it is an illusion to believe that one can inhabit multiple cultures in a deep sense. Immigrants know that there are hard choices to be made, and these have benefits as well as costs. The immigrant who falls in love and wants to marry outside his ethnic and religious group knows that, in doing so, he might be risking his relationship with his family. The newcomer who wants to become an American is embarking on a journey that is likely to cut him off from his native country, so that he becomes a stranger to people he has grown up with. Some immigrants never manage this transition between cultures, occupying a tragic middle position in which they are at home neither in America nor in their homeland.

Even so, on some issues there are immense practical advantages to adopting the American way. The best example of this is speaking English. I have heard bilingual activists deny that speaking English is a prerequisite to enjoying the American dream. One Latino activist informed me that Cubans can get along very well in Miami without speaking a word of English: you can work for a Cuban company, shop at Cuban stores, make a deposit at a Cuban bank, read Spanish-language newspapers, and so on. But even in this exceptional case, you can flourish only if you stay in Miami. By and large, immigrants reject the harmful doctrines of the bilingual activists. The vast majority of immigrants understand perfectly well that they cannot enjoy a full life in the United States unless they can speak English.

Many conservatives have expressed concerns about the balkanization of America. The multicultural dream is their nightmare. Even though I agree that balkanization is undesirable, I do not share the conservatives' pessimism. I know that America is not, and never will be, Bosnia. I recognize the power of the American idea and the strength of the solvent of Americanization. Consider a typical Indian woman at JFK Airport. To look at her—the sari, the beads, the dot on her forehead, and so on—she seems utterly out of place in a modern, Western civilization. But then look at her four-year-old son. The little fellow is running around, he is making a big noise, he is biting people—in short, he has been thoroughly Americanized. However fiercely the first-generation immigrant holds onto the native culture, I do not believe that he can prevent his children from being assimilated.

In general, I believe that this is a good thing, but it is not an unmixed blessing. There are some respects in which I do not want my daughter to be completely Americanized. I have noticed that when second-generation Asian-Americans become fully assimilated, they don't study as hard and their test scores fall. I am quite willing to let my daughter date and choose the person she wants to marry, as long as the process begins at the age of thirty. I am currently doing Internet research into convent schools. "Good luck," my American friends say sarcastically, and of course they are right. What are the chances that my effort to thwart full assimilation will succeed? Not very good. But I still intend to try. So wish me luck: I will need it.

CHAPTER FOUR

THE REPARATIONS FALLACY

What African–Americans Owe America

Other revolutions have been the insurrection of the
oppressed; this was the repentance of the tyrant.

—EMERSON

I T SEEMS CLEAR THAT AMERICA WORKS PRETTY WELL FOR
immigrants, but does it also work well for domestic minority
groups, such as African-Americans? This was a topic on
which I debated the Reverend Jesse Jackson a few years ago at
Stanford University. Jackson began by asserting that America is
and always has been a racist society. To demonstrate this, Jackson
evoked the painful history of slavery and segregation. He also cited
a contemporary list of horrors—the Rodney King beating, the role
of Mark Fuhrman in the O. J. Simpson case, racist comments at
Texaco, the blacks who couldn't get served at Denny's, and several other examples of continuing racism against black Americans.

I did not deny that racism exists, and conceded that in a big
country like the United States one could find many examples of
it. But I asked Jackson to prove to me that racism today was

potent enough and widespread enough that it could prevent me, or him, or my daughter, or his children, from achieving their basic aspirations? Where is that kind of racism, I said—show it to me. Jackson hemmed and hawed, wrinkled his forehead, played with his mustache. He was thinking deeply.

Finally he admitted that he could provide no such evidence. But its absence, he went on to argue, in no way demonstrated that racism had abated. No, America was in his view just as racist as in the past. The only difference is that racism has gone underground; it has become institutionalized, so that in an invisible but no less insidious way, it continues to thwart blacks and other minorities from achieving the American dream. "Racism used to be overt," Jackson said. "Now it is covert." He went into a rhyme sequence. "I may be well dressed, but I'm still oppressed." And so on.

I found the concept of this rich, successful man—who arrived by private jet, who speaks at the Democratic National Convention, whose son is a congressman—identifying himself as a victim of oppression a bit puzzling and amusing. But I suppressed the urge to chuckle. I reminded myself that Jackson's indignation was quite genuine, and that I was witnessing a clash between two perspectives, what may be termed the immigrant perspective and that of the leadership of indigenous minority groups. I use the term "indigenous" loosely to refer to African-Americans and American Indians. These are groups that have been in America even longer than most European immigrants.

That there is a clash of views between immigrants and indigenous minorities will come as news to some advocates of multiculturalism, who like to portray nonwhites, women, and homosexuals as allied in a grand coalition against that oppressive enemy of humanity, the white male heterosexual. There are many problems with this morality tale, but perhaps the most serious is that non-white immigrants and indigenous minorities see America very differently. Ideologically, if not geographically, they are poles apart.

Immigrants today are mostly "people of color": this they have in common with African-Americans. But this is where the similarity ends. The immigrant comes here from South Korea, Nigeria, or the West Indies and finds America to be a terrific place. Then he runs into the likes of Jesse Jackson, who tell him that he is completely wrong, he doesn't know anything, he should stick around for a while, he will soon discover the baleful influence of racism.

Why, then, do nonwhite immigrants and the leadership of indigenous minority groups see America so differently? The immigrant typically compares America to his home country. "In Nicaragua I have to work for $6 a day. You mean that McDonald's will pay me $6 an hour? Where do I sign up for overtime?" By this comparative or historical standard, America comes off looking good. Patriotism comes easily to the immigrant who has chosen to become an American.

African-American leaders, by contrast, use a utopian standard in judging the United States. Their argument is not that the United States is a worse place for them to live than Haiti or Ethiopia, but that the United States falls short in comparison to the Garden of Eden. "Why should I work for $6 an hour? That's slave labor. Look at the guy in the high-rise office building who gets $75 an hour. If I'm not making as much as he is, then I am oppressed." This is a very different psychology.

So who is right: the immigrants, who have come recently, or the indigenous minorities, who have been here a long time? In our debate, Jackson addressed this question by pointing out that African-Americans could not be compared with immigrants, because the immigrants for the most part came voluntarily, while African-Americans came to the United States in chains. This is a good point, although its contemporary relevance is unclear. Jackson also said that earlier generations of immigrants—the Jews, the Irish, and the Italians—could easily assimilate because they were white. Blacks, he added, don't have this option.

This argument seems reasonable, but it relies for its plausibility on anachronism. Today we often have trouble distinguishing between members of ethnic groups from various parts of Europe. This, however, is only because of their high rates of intermarriage. But intermarriage between Irish-Americans and Italian-Americans, or between Protestants and Catholics, or between Christians and Jews, has only become popular in recent years. In 1850 it was quite easy to identify an Irish immigrant. That's the only way "No Irish Need Apply" rules could be enforced.[1]

So the notion that the old immigrants had it easy because they could pass for white is wrong. Indeed, the experience of new generations of immigrants—the Chinese, the Pakistanis, the Cubans, the Nigerians—is virtually identical to that of earlier generations of European immigrants. The problems of the newcomers—difficulties with the English language, lack of credit, a feeling of isolation—are precisely the problems that the Irish, the Italians, and the Jews had. True, it is easier to identify a Pakistani than an Italian, but what does this prove? Prejudice and hostility against the European immigrants was vastly *greater* than anything endured by today's Asian, African, and Latin American immigrants.

Indigenous minorities, then, are a special case. They, not the immigrants, are the moral and political force behind the multicultural agenda. They are the ones pressing for multicultural education, and racial preferences, and reparations. African-Americans and American Indians are the only groups for whom patriotism is a problem. I do not mean this in an accusatory way; theirs is the natural ambivalence of any people who are deeply convinced that their life in America has been shaped by oppression.

For instance, it is commonplace among American Indians that the white man arrived on these shores with an incorrigible bigotry toward native peoples and then put into effect a policy of exterminating the Indian population. If "America" represents a country that is guilty of unmitigated hatred and genocide, how can the native Indians who were victims of this viciousness and slaughter be expected to salute the flag and sing "God Bless America"? If the white man is guilty as charged, they obviously cannot.

But is the white man guilty as charged? Even on the count of racism against Indians, the evidence is ambiguous. Many whites considered blacks to be racially inferior but they did not feel the same way about American Indians. In this respect Thomas Jefferson is typical: while entertaining doubts that blacks were as intelligent as whites, he confidently stated that any backwardness on the part of the Indian was entirely the result of circumstance.[2] True, the white man frequently portrayed the Indian as a "noble savage," but the accent here is on the word *noble*. There is a long tradition in the West of admiring the noble savage as harkening from an age of innocence, before the corruptions introduced by civilization.[3] It is highly significant that several leading figures during the founding period (Patrick Henry, John Marshall, Thomas Jefferson) proposed intermarriage between whites and native Indians as a way to integrate the Indians into the mainstream. "What they thought impossible with respect to blacks," political scientist Ralph Lerner writes, "was seen as highly desirable with respect to Indians."[4]

But this is just talk about the white man's feelings; we also need to discuss the white man's actions toward the native Indians. Aren't the European settlers guilty of genocide? As a matter of fact, they are not. Millions of Indians perished as a result of contact with the white man, but for the most part they died by contracting his diseases: smallpox, measles, malaria, tuberculosis. There are isolated instances of European military commanders attempting to vanquish hostile Indian tribes by giving them smallpox-infected blankets. But as William McNeill documents in *Plagues and Peoples*, the white man generally transmitted his diseases to the Indians without knowing it, and the Indians died in large numbers because they had not developed immunities to those diseases. This is tragedy on a grand scale, but it is not genocide, because genocide implies an *intention* to wipe out an entire population. McNeill points out that, a few centuries earlier, Europeans themselves contracted lethal diseases, including the bubonic plague, from Mongol invaders from the Asian steppes. The Europeans didn't have immunities, and the plague decimated one-third of the population of Europe.[5] Despite the magnitude of deaths and suffering, no one calls this genocide, and they are right not to do so.

None of this is to excuse the settlers' injustices, or to diminish the historical misfortune of the American Indians. In his famous "Essay on the Three Races," Tocqueville contrasts the situation of the native Indian with that of blacks. Tocqueville's essay makes revealing reading because we are taught by multicultural educators to regard the circumstances of blacks and native Indians as very similar: both suffered miserably at the hands of the white man. But Tocqueville captures a nuance that has eluded our present-day ideologues. The Indian, he writes, never wanted Western civilization, but the white man was determined to shove it down his throat. In short, the Indian is faced with the problem of *forced inclusion*. Blacks, Tocqueville said, want nothing more than to share the privileges of white society, but whites will not allow them to do so. In short, blacks are faced with the problem of *forced exclusion*.

The charge of forced exclusion is the more serious one, and in this chapter I focus on African-Americans. Most blacks believe that they have suffered, and continue to suffer, terrible injustice at the hands of the white man. The great black scholar W. E. B. DuBois said his life in America was defined by a kind of double consciousness, resulting in a divided loyalty. DuBois wrote, "One ever feels this two-ness: an American, a Negro; two souls, two thoughts, two unreconciled strivings; two warring ideals in one dark body, whose dogged strength alone keeps it from being torn asunder."[6]

The problem of patriotism for black Americans was even more dramatically stated in the late nineteenth century by the black abolitionist Frederick Douglass. "This fourth of July," he said, "is yours, not mine. You may rejoice, I must mourn. To drag a man in fetters into the grand illuminated temple of liberty, and call upon him to join you in joyous anthems, were inhuman mockery and sacrilegious irony. I have no patriotism. I have no country. What country have I? The institutions of this country do not know me, do not recognize me as a man. I have not—I cannot have—any love for this country, as such, or for its constitution. I desire to see its overthrow as speedily as possible."[7] Douglass's statement borders on treason, yet it is an honorable treason. His argument is one that Aristotle would recognize. What he is saying is that one cannot be a good citizen in a bad country.

The United States military is disproportionately made up of black Americans. These men and women are apparently ready and willing to fight for their country, but it is not unreasonable to wonder why. If Douglass is right, this is not their country, it has not treated them well, it continues to treat them badly, so they are at best (as the popular T-shirt has it) "Africans in America." To speak in the language of Malcolm X, are blacks in the armed forces nothing more than "house Negroes" foolishly risking their lives to protect the master's plantation? This seems a very harsh assessment, but it is undoubtedly true that there is very little in the black literary tradition, and very little said by contemporary black leaders, that makes the case for why black Americans should love America and fight for America. Why, then, should they?

Leading black scholars such as John Hope Franklin say that the problems of African-Americans go back to the beginning—to the American founding. Franklin argues that the founders "betrayed the ideals to which they gave lip service." They wrote "eloquently at one moment for the brotherhood of man and in the next moment denied it to their black brothers." They chose to "degrade the human spirit by equating five black men with three white men." The consequences have been unremittingly painful for African-Americans. "Having created a tragically flawed revolutionary doctrine and a Constitution that did not bestow the blessings of liberty on its posterity, the founding fathers set the stage for every succeeding generation to apologize, compromise, and temporize on those principles of liberty that were supposed to be the very foundation of our system of government and way of life."[8]

Such views have become commonplace among African-Americans, and they are routinely promulgated in multicultural textbooks. Interestingly Franklin's criticism of the founders relies on the same reasoning that Justice Taney relied on in the infamous *Dred Scott* decision. Writing for the majority in this notorious 1857 case upholding slavery, Taney argued that since several of the founders, including Jefferson, were slave owners, these men could not have really meant that "all men are created equal." They may have written "all men," but what they really meant was "white men." As for black slaves, Taney concluded that they have "no rights that the white man is bound to respect."[9]

Are Franklin and Taney right? Are the founders guilty as alleged? Let us consider the evidence fairly, beginning with the notorious "three-fifths" clause to which Franklin alludes. To the modern mind, this is one of the most troubling pieces of evidence against the founders. And yet it should not be, because the clause itself has nothing to say about the intrinsic worth of blacks.

The origins of the clause are to be found in the debate between the northern states and the southern states over the issue of political representation. The South wanted to count blacks as whole persons, in order to increase its political power. The North wanted blacks to count for nothing—not for the purpose of rejecting their humanity, but in order to preserve and strengthen the antislavery majority in Congress. It was not a proslavery southerner but an antislavery northerner, James Wilson of Pennsylvania, who proposed the three-fifths compromise. The effect was to limit the South's political representation and its ability to protect the institution of slavery. Frederick Douglass understood this: he called the three-fifths clause "a downright disability laid upon the slaveholding states" which deprived them of "two-fifths of their natural basis of representation."[10] So a provision of the Constitution that was antislavery and pro-black in intent as well as in effect is today cited to prove that the American founders championed the cause of racist oppression.

Refuting the myth that the three-fifths clause degrades black humanity does not absolve the founders of the charge of hypocrisy. We still have to meet Franklin and Taney's argument that the founders claimed to be antislavery while approving a Constitution that permitted the continuation of slavery. Despite Jefferson's impressive fulminations against slavery, the fact remains that he owned some two hundred slaves and did not free them. Does it not follow that the author of "all men are created equal" could not have meant what he said?

It should not be surprising that Jefferson, a Virginia planter, owned slaves; in this he was a man of his time. What is surprising is that, as a southern slave owner, Jefferson made no attempt to justify slavery by contending that it was good for the slave. On the contrary, he repeatedly denounced slavery in the strongest terms. Even if blacks could be shown to be intellectually inferior to whites, Jefferson denied that this would provide a just basis for their enslavement. "Whatever be their talents, it is no measure of their rights."[11] Jefferson was one of the least religious of the founders, but strikingly he consistently adopted prophetic biblical language in condemning slavery. "I tremble for my country when I reflect that God is just, that His justice cannot sleep forever."[12]

Given Jefferson's firm repudiation of slavery, a view shared by most of the framers, why didn't these men move rapidly to free their slaves and insist upon a Constitution that would immediately secure equal rights for all? To answer this question, we must understand something about the relationship between slavery and democracy, and about the practical dilemma faced by the framers in Philadelphia.

For millennia, slavery was an accepted part of society. In numerous civilizations both Western and non-Western, slavery needed no defenders because it had no critics. The major religions of the world, including Christianity and Islam, permitted slavery. True, Christianity and Islam both hold that all persons are equal in God's sight. But for centuries this was considered a spiritual truth, inapplicable to the hierarchies of this world. But starting in the seventeenth century, certain segments of Christianity—initially the Quakers, then the evangelical Christians—began to interpret biblical equality as forbidding the ownership of one man by another. Only then, for the first time, did slavery become a political problem.[13]

Before that, slaves were typically captured in warfare or bought and sold in slave markets, and the greatest thinkers of antiquity condoned slavery. Aristotle distinguished between those who were "slaves by nature," i.e., those who lacked the mental capacity to rule themselves, and "slaves by convention," i.e., those who had the misfortune to be captured and enslaved. While Aristotle did not attempt to defend conventional slavery in terms of justice, he did allow it on grounds of expediency. In every society, he said, there is dirty work to be done, and someone has to do it. If slaves do the hard labor, Aristotle theorized, then there would be leisure for others to engage in higher pursuits like art and philosophy and politics.

In his debate with Abraham Lincoln in the mid–nineteenth century, Stephen Douglas offered a version of the Aristotelian argument in defense of the slave system of the American South. "The civilized world has always held that when any race of men have shown themselves to be so degraded by ignorance, superstition, cruelty, and barbarism, as to be utterly incapable of governing themselves, they must, in the nature of things, be governed by others, by such laws as are deemed to be applicable to their condition."[14] The careful reader will also recognize in this statement echoes of Plato's argument for why the wise should rule.

We might regard Stephen Douglas's argument to be crude and despicable, but Abraham Lincoln did not. He agreed with Douglas: it is absurd to construct a regime in which the foolish are in charge. Thus democracy poses a problem that the American founders and Lincoln all recognized: how can the wise—who are by definition the few—be reliably identified and chosen to rule by the many? Representative government is based on the hope that the majority will exercise their power on behalf of right—that they will choose others to govern who are wiser than themselves. Yet modern democracy introduces a crucial qualification to the claim of the wise to rule: such rule is only legitimate when it is vindicated by popular consent. The requirement of consent is necessary to ensure that the wise do not rule simply for their own benefit, but also for the benefit of the unwise.

"The only distinction between freedom and slavery," Alexander Hamilton wrote, "consists in this: in the former state, a man is governed by laws to which he has given his consent; in the latter, he is governed by the will of another."[15] Here we can see what the American founders saw instantly: that the argument for democracy and the argument against slavery are one and the same. Both are based on the political doctrine that no man may rule another man without his consent.

Since blacks are human beings, slavery is against natural right and should be prohibited. But how? Here is where Jefferson and the founders faced two profound obstacles. The first was that virtually all of them recognized the degraded condition of blacks in America and understood it posed a formidable hurdle to granting blacks the rights of citizenship. By contrast with monarchy and aristocracy, which only require subjects to obey, self-government requires citizens who have the capacity to be rulers. Jefferson and the founders were legitimately concerned that a group that had been enslaved for centuries was not ready to assume the responsibility of democratic self-rule.

Jefferson was also aware of the existence of intense and widespread white prejudices against blacks which, whatever their cause, seemed to prevent the two peoples from coexisting harmoniously on the same soil. Madison, who shared this view, developed a plan for the U.S. government to raise money to repatriate blacks to Africa. These so-called colonization schemes seem bizarre today, but in the eighteenth century they were supported by many abolitionists, white as well as black. Lincoln himself echoed Jefferson's concerns, and prior to the Civil War he endorsed colonization as a way for blacks to live free and unmolested in a country of their own.

The deference of Jefferson and the American founders to popular prejudices strikes many contemporary scholars as an intellectual and moral scandal. Some, like John Hope Franklin, suggest that popular convictions simply represented a frustrating obstacle that the founders should have dealt with resolutely and uncompromisingly. But in a democratic society, the absence of the people's agreement on a fundamental question of governance is no mere technicality. The case for democracy, no less than the case against slavery, rests on the legitimacy of the people's consent. To outlaw slavery without the consent of the majority of whites would be to destroy democracy, indeed to destroy the very basis for outlawing slavery itself.

The men gathered in Philadelphia were in a peculiar predicament. For them to sanction slavery would be to proclaim the illegitimacy of the American revolution and the new form of government based on the people's consent; yet for them to outlaw slavery without securing the people's consent would have the same effect. In practical terms as well, the choice facing the founders was not to permit or to prohibit slavery. Rather, the choice was either to establish a union in which slavery was tolerated, or not to have a union at all. Any suggestion that the southern states could have been persuaded to join a union and give up slavery can be dismissed as preposterous. As Harry Jaffa puts it, had the founders insisted upon securing *all* the rights of *all* men, they would have ended up securing *no* rights for *anybody.*[16]

Thus the accusation that the founders compromised on the Declaration's principle that "all men are created equal" for the purpose of expediency reflects a grave misunderstanding. The founders were confronted with a competing principle that is also present in the Declaration: governments derive their legitimacy from the "consent of the governed." Both principles must be satisfied, and when they cannot be, compromise is not merely permissible but morally required.

The framers found a middle ground, not between principle and practice, but between opposition to slavery and majority consent. They produced a Constitution in which the concept of slavery is tolerated in deference to consent, but not given any moral approval in recognition of the slave's natural rights. Nowhere in the document is the term "slavery" used. Slaves are always described as "persons," implying their possession of natural rights. The founders were also careful to approve a Constitution that refuses to acknowledge the existence of racial distinctions, thus producing a document that transcended its time.

None of the supposed contradictions that contemporary scholars have located in the founding documents were unrecognized by the founders. Many of the framers justified their toleration of slavery on prudential grounds, for in the 1770s and 1780s they had reason to believe that slavery was losing its commercial appeal. In this they were wrong, because Eli Whitney's invention of the cotton gin in 1793 (which the founders could not have anticipated) revived the demand for slavery in the South.

Even so, the test of the founders' project is the practical consequence: did the founding strengthen or weaken the institution of slavery? The American Revolution should be judged by its consequences. Before 1776, slavery was legal in every state in America. Yet by 1804 every state north of Maryland had abolished slavery either immediately or gradually; southern and border states prohibited further slave importations from abroad; and Congress was committed to outlawing the slave trade in 1808, which it did. Slavery was no longer a national but a sectional institution, and one under moral and political siege.

Abraham Lincoln not only perceived the founders' dilemma, he inherited it. The principle of popular rule is based on Jefferson's doctrine that "all men are created equal," yet the greatest crisis in American history arose when the people denied that "all men are created equal" and in so doing denied the basis of their own legitimacy. Lincoln had two choices: work to overthrow democracy, or work to secure consent through persuasion. Conscious that he, too, must defer, as the founders did, to prevailing prejudices, Lincoln nevertheless sought to neutralize those prejudices so they did not become a barrier to securing black freedom. In a series of artfully conditional claims—"If God gave the black man little, that little let him enjoy"—Lincoln paid ritual obeisance to existing racism while drawing even racists into his coalition to end slavery. He made these rhetorical concessions because he knew that the possibility for securing antislavery consent was far better in his time than in the 1780s.

Commenting on the Declaration of Independence, Lincoln said of the founders: "They intended to include all men, but they did not intend to declare all men equal in all respects. They defined with tolerable distinctness in what respects they did consider all men created equal—equal in certain inalienable rights. They did not mean to assert the obvious untruth, that all were then actually enjoying that equality, nor yet, that they were about to confer it immediately upon them. They meant simply to declare the *right,* so that the *enforcement* of it must follow as fast as circumstances should permit."[17] By working through, rather than around, the democratic process, Lincoln justified the nation's faith in the untried experiment of representative self-government. In vindicating the slave's right to rule himself, Lincoln also vindicated the legitimacy of democratic self-rule. Thus it is accurate to say that Lincoln gave America a "new birth of freedom."

Lincoln's position came to be shared by Frederick Douglass, who had once denounced the Constitution but who eventually reached the conclusion that it contained antislavery principles. "Abolish slavery tomorrow, and not a sentence or syllable of the Constitution needs to be altered," Douglass said. Slavery, he concluded, was merely "scaffolding to the magnificent structure, to be removed as soon as the building was completed."[18] Douglass came to understand what contemporary multiculturalists apparently do not—that the best antislavery program is not necessarily support for the grandest impractical scheme but rather "is that which deals the deadliest blow upon slavery that can be given at a particular time."[19]

It took a civil war to destroy slavery, and more than half a million whites were killed in that war, "one life for every six slaves freed," C. Vann Woodward reminds us. But for Lincoln as for Douglass, the greatest white and black statesmen of the time, the triumph of the union and the emancipation of the slaves represented not the victory of might over right, but the reverse. Justice had won out over expediency, and the principles of the American founding had at long last been realized. The founders exercised wisdom and prudence in producing a charter for a society immeasurably better than the one in which they found themselves. History has vindicated their philosophical statesmanship. Black Americans and indeed all of us owe the American founders a profound debt of gratitude.

Having examined the issue of slavery, let us now discuss racism. Racism is a doctrine of innate or biological superiority. In its classic form, it leads to discrimination, which deprives members of victimized groups the equal protection of the laws. While slavery ended in the United States nearly a century and a half ago, racism continues to exist. Many African-American leaders insist that it is as bad as, if not worse than, it ever was. "Racism is as healthy today as it was during the Enlightenment," says Nobel laureate Toni Morrison.[20] "Racism is an integral, permanent and indestructible component of this society," writes legal scholar Derrick Bell.[21] These writers hold societal racism responsible for the current problems of blacks. Is America to blame because African-Americans are not doing as well as members of other groups?

As an immigrant, I am constantly surprised by how much I hear racism talked about and how little I actually see it. (Even fewer are the incidents in which I have experienced it directly.)

When one examines the policies of universities, companies, and the government, one finds that they actually discriminate *in favor* of African-Americans and other minority groups, and against white males. Socially most Americans go out of their way to cater to, and to avoid offending, blacks. Such measures seem unlikely in a racist society. There are specific incidents of racism and specific victims, to be sure, but the very fact that we can identify them proves that they are not typical, and the ensuing outcry shows the degree to which racism has become stigmatized in American society.

For the past several years I have been speaking at American colleges on the issue of affirmative action. Inevitably some student or professor will harangue me about how indispensable racial preferences are at that particular school because of the pervasiveness of racism and discrimination. I then ask, "Do you know of any bigots in your admissions office who are trying to keep blacks and Hispanics out?" Not once has my question led to the identification of any bigots.

Where, then, is the racism? At this point my interlocutor typically makes the Jesse Jackson maneuver: having failed to locate overt racism, he insists upon the pervasiveness of covert racism. The absence of individual racism inspires the allegation of "institutional racism." And in this case the culprit is the admissions standard used by the selective college to decide who gets in. In particular, the villain of the story turns out to be the Scholastic Assessment Test (SAT). This test, we hear, is racially and culturally biased.

I took the SAT myself in the late 1970s, and it didn't seem to me that it had been prepared by the Ku Klux Klan. The SAT seeks to measure verbal ability, reading comprehension, mathematical skill, and logical and reasoning aptitude, all of which seem quite relevant to performing well in college. It is conceivable that some questions on the verbal section of the test are biased, in that they refer to material outside the normal experience of inner-city blacks. But let us focus, for a moment, on the math section. The typical question goes like this: "If an automobile can go at a speed of 75 miles per hour, how far can it go in 40 minutes?" No one can maintain with a straight face that simple equations are racially biased, or that algebra is rigged against Hispanics. Yet the performance gaps between blacks and whites are greater on the math section than on the verbal section.

What this suggests is that the test is accurately measuring not innate capacity but differences of academic performance. And on those measures of merit that selective colleges typically use, not all racial groups do equally well. So far I have focused on a single test, so let me expand my argument by asking you to envision any test that measures intellectual achievement or economic performance. It may be a reading test given to six-year-olds, or a math test given to fifteen-year-olds, or the law school admission test, or the graduate record exam, or the business school test, or the firefighters test, or the police sergeant test, or the civil service exam. It doesn't matter—you name the test. Now if your chosen test is today administered to a hundred randomly selected members from each of four groups—white, black, Hispanic, and Asian-American—I will tell you in advance the result. Whites and Asians will do the best, Hispanics will fall in the middle, and African-Americans, alas, will do the least well.

For the past several years, I have challenged leading African-American scholars to give me a single example of a test that violates the pattern of results that I have identified here. None of them have been able to do so. This is a serious problem for those who blame racial bias for the comparatively poor test results of African-Americans. It is conceivable that this test or that test is flawed or biased, but to maintain that every test, in every subject, in every part of the country, is conspiratorially biased in the same way—this is absurd.

The simple truth is that merit, not racism, is responsible for performance differences on the test. Merit, not racism, is the primary obstacle to enrolling larger numbers of blacks and Hispanics in selective universities. This realization has come as a surprise to many leaders of the civil rights movement. In the 1950s and 1960s, Martin Luther King Jr. championed the cause of merit against that of nepotism and racial favoritism. All we are asking, King said, is that we be judged on our merits as individuals, based on the content of our character and not the color of our skins.

Eventually the leaders of the United States agreed to this. There were strong pockets of resistance, especially in the South, but the heroic persistence of King and his supporters was vindicated. There was a series of landmark rulings and laws—*Brown v. Board of Education,* the Civil Rights Act of 1964, the Voting Rights Act, the Fair Housing Bill—which established equality of rights under the law for all citizens. Merit became the operating standard, just as King demanded. King fully expected that merit would produce diversity and that equality of rights for individuals would lead to equality of results for groups.

It has been a generation since King's death, and we now see that King's premise was false. Equality of rights for individuals has not led to equality of results for groups. Merit, like racism, produces inequality. And inequalities produced by merit are far more justifiable than inequalities produced by favoritism or racism. Consider the example of the National Basketball Association. African-Americans are 12 percent of the population but more than 75 percent of NBA players. Why, then, do we not hear demands for more Jews and Asians to be represented on the courts? Presumably because it is merit that is producing this racially disproportionate result. If coaches are picking the best dribblers and passers and shooters, then who cares if one group has more players and another group has less?

If this seems like a sensible approach, it should also be applied to universities, and corporations, and government jobs. But here the civil rights leaders face a nightmare scenario. They know that merit standards, applied in a neutral or color-blind way, are likely to result in a kind of racial hierarchy, with blacks at the bottom. The prospect of this upsets many blacks and embarrasses many whites. Racial preferences are a way to appease black discontent and reduce white embarrassment. They have nothing to do with fighting racism. Not a single one of the black or Hispanic students preferentially admitted to colleges over the years has shown that he or she has been victimized by racism. Nor have any of the white and Asian students who have been turned away, despite better grades, test scores, and extracurricular talents, been shown to have discriminated against anyone.

A just social policy seeks to benefit those who have been harmed and impose the cost on those who have done the harming. This is not what racial preference policies do. They seek to camouflage the performance differences between racial groups and to benefit less-qualified members of some groups at the expense of more-qualified members of other groups. By applying two different standards—a higher one to Asians and whites, and a lower one to blacks and Hispanics—admissions officers and corporate recruiters can show a diverse outcome and pretend that all groups are performing equally well. The racial caste society is averted, but at the expense of undermining two bedrock American principles—the principle of merit and the principle of equal rights under the law.

Preferences create the illusion that blacks are competitive with whites, but wouldn't it be better for blacks in fact to be competitive with whites? To see how this could be possible, we must candidly discuss the reasons for the merit gap. Why is it the case that on virtually every measure of academic ability and economic performance, African-Americans do poorly in comparison with other groups? In this debate there are three positions.

The first position can be identified with *The Bell Curve,* the controversial book by Richard Herrnstein and Charles Murray. In it the authors contend that there may be natural, biological differences between the races that account for their unequal levels of performance.[22] *The Bell Curve* was written as an argument against racial preferences, although to my mind it offers the strongest possible argument in *support* of such preferences. After all, if group differences are large, innate, and ineradicable, then the only alternative to a racial caste society is to set up multiple measures of performance (a kind of Special Olympics) so that all groups can enjoy a measure of reward and recognition. Let us call the argument advanced by Herrnstein and Murray the genetic position.

The genetic position has been challenged, for the better part of a century, by what may be termed the liberal position. The liberal position, argued by scholars such as Andrew Hacker, Christopher Jencks, and William Julius Wilson, says that the reason for group differences in academic achievement and economic performance is that society artificially creates such differences. In this view, societal oppression, and specifically racism, causes group inequalities that otherwise would not exist.

The genetic and the liberal view have been at odds for decades, and they operate like a seesaw: when one is up, the other is down. In the early part of the twentieth century, the genetic view was predominant. Most people assumed that there were natural differences between groups that explained why some did better than others. But in the 1950s and 1960s, the genetic view came under sustained assault. The liberals said: How can you say that blacks are doing poorly due to some supposed natural deficit? Look at all the discrimination to which they are subjected. This argument was entirely plausible, which is why the genetic view began to lose support and the liberal view became the conventional wisdom.

Today, however, the liberal view has become intellectually bankrupt. To see why this is so, consider the SAT. Both on the verbal and the math section of the test, Asian-Americans and whites who come from poor families—let us say, families earning below $20,000 a year—score higher than African-Americans who come from well-off families—say, families earning over $60,000 a year.[23] This fact, which is easy to verify and is not denied by any informed person in the race debate, destroys the old canard that tests are mere calibrators of socioeconomic privilege. But it also poses a grave challenge to the liberal position itself. Recall that the liberal view attributes group differences in performance to racism. But how could racism operate in such a way that it enables poor whites and Asians to score higher on math tests than upper-middle-class African-Americans? When I pose this question to liberal scholars, they usually call me insulting names.

So the debate is at a tragic standoff between two unacceptable alternatives: the genetic position and the liberal position. To break the deadlock, a group of scholars—including Thomas Sowell, Orlando Patterson, and Shelby Steele—has offered a third position that I support. This may be called the cultural position. This view holds that there are cultural, which is to say *behavioral,* differences between groups. These are observable in everyday life, they can be measured by the usual techniques of social science, and they can be directly related to academic achievement and economic success.

A few years ago sociologist Sanford Dornbusch and his colleagues were puzzled by the persistence of large differences in academic performance between Asian-Americans and African-Americans. They were disturbed by the possibility that these differences might be due to natural or genetic factors. So Dornbusch and his colleagues conducted a comparative study of white, black, Hispanic, and Asian-American students. Here is what they found: "In general Asian-American students devote relatively more time to their studies, are more likely to attribute their success to hard work, and are more likely to report that their parents have high standards for school performance....In contrast, African-American and Hispanic students are more cavalier about the consequences of poor school performance, devote less time to their studies, are less likely than others to attribute their success to hard work, and report that their parents have relatively lower standards."[24]

Obviously this doesn't settle the issue; one may ask, "But why do Asian-Americans and African-Americans show these differences in attitude and behavior?" Undoubtedly many complex factors are involved, but one that is worth mentioning is the two-parent family. It seems obvious that two parents will have, on average, more time than a single parent to invest in a child's upbringing, discipline, homework supervision, and so on. What is the illegitimacy rate in the Asian-American community? Less than 5 percent. In the African-American community? Nearly 70 percent!

I mentioned these facts at a recent conference, and one of my fellow panelists erupted in anger. "Yes, but who do you think caused the decline of the black family? Clearly it is the result of slavery." He went on to remind me that in no southern state were slaves legally permitted to marry and that masters periodically broke up families and sold off children. All of this is sadly true. And the argument sounds so reasonable that it is only by looking at the facts that we see that it is largely erroneous. In the early part of the twentieth century W. E. B. DuBois published his study of the black family in which he pointed out that the illegitimacy rate for blacks in the United States was around 20 percent.[25] From 1900 to 1965 the black illegitimacy rate remained roughly at that figure.[26] Indeed, in 1965 Daniel Patrick Moynihan did his famous report on the Negro family and announced a national scandal: the black illegitimacy rate had reached 25 percent.[27]

Let us concede that slavery was primarily responsible for that figure. After emancipation, however, African-Americans made strenuous attempts to reunite and rebuild their families. This is a black success story that is not well known. (Black activists don't publicize it because it disrupts the profitable narrative of victimization.) Ironically, it is during the period from 1965 to the present—a period that saw the Great Society, the civil rights laws, affirmative action, welfare, and other attempts to integrate blacks into the mainstream and raise their standard of living— that the black family disintegrated. Today that disintegration has reached the point that the typical African-American child is born out of wedlock.

The African-American sociologist William Julius Wilson concedes the existence of cultural pathologies like illegitimacy and high crime rates in the black community. He blames these not on slavery but on racism, poverty, and unemployment.[28] Wilson points out, for example, that a young black man who doesn't have a job is in no position to support a family. Who should be surprised, therefore, that he gets a girl pregnant and refuses to marry her? The problem with Wilson's analysis is that it ignores the historical record. Consider the period of the 1930s in the segregationist South. Racism, poverty, and unemployment were rampant. Yet what was the black illegitimacy rate? It remained at 20 percent! The black crime rate? It was a lot lower than it is now. Neither Wilson nor anyone else has explained why, at a time when economic and social conditions have greatly improved for blacks, these cultural problems have worsened.

☆ ☆ ☆

Let me summarize my argument by reexamining the debate in the early twentieth century between W. E. B. DuBois and Booker T. Washington. Although the debate focused on black Americans, it is relevant to the question of how any group starting out at the bottom can advance in society. DuBois, a distinguished scholar and cofounder of the National Association for the Advancement of Colored People (NAACP), argued that African-Americans in the United States face one big problem, and it is racism. Washington, who was born a slave but went on to become head of the Tuskegee Institute, maintained that African-Americans face two big problems. One is racism, he conceded. The other, he said, is black cultural disadvantage. Washington said that black crime rates were too high, black savings rates were too low, blacks did not have enough respect for educational achievement.

DuBois countered that these problems, if they existed, were due to the legacy of slavery and racism. Washington did not disagree, but he insisted that, whatever their source, these cultural problems demanded attention. What is the point of having rights, Washington said, without the ability to exercise those rights and compete effectively with other groups? To put the matter in contemporary terms, there is little benefit in having the right to a job at General Motors if you don't know how to do the job. Washington further argued that if these cultural deficiencies were not addressed, they would help to *strengthen* racism by giving it an empirical foundation.

The civil rights movement, led by the NAACP, fought for decades to implement the DuBois program and secure basic rights for black Americans. This was a necessary campaign, and ultimately it was successful. The laws were changed, and blacks achieved their goal of full citizenship. Obviously enforcement remained an issue, but at this point, it seems to me, the DuBois program was largely achieved. At this crucial juncture the civil rights movement should have moved from the DuBois agenda to the Booker T. Washington agenda.

Unfortunately, this did not happen. It still hasn't happened. Even today the NAACP and other civil rights groups continue to "agitate, agitate, agitate" to achieve black progress. This is the approach that Jesse Jackson has perfected. It draws on the language and tactics of political struggle to make gains. But how significant are those gains? A few years ago I was in Washington, D.C., and there was a big march on the mall. All the major civil rights groups were represented. Several speakers ascended the podium, thumped their fists, and said, "We've got to go to Bill Clinton and demand 300,000 new jobs." Now this was during the impeachment controversy, and anyone who had been following the news knew that Bill Clinton had found it incredibly difficult to get *one* job—for Monica Lewinsky. Where did the man have 300,000 jobs to give anyone? The fact is that the civil rights leadership continues to pursue a strategy that has run its course, that no longer pays real dividends.

Meanwhile, there is another group that is following the Booker T. Washington strategy, and that is the nonwhite immigrants. I don't mean just the Koreans and the Asian Indians; I also mean black immigrants—the West Indians, the Haitians, the Nigerians. All are darker than African-Americans, and yet white racism does not seem to stop them. The immigrants know that racism today is not systematic, it is episodic, and they are able to find ways to navigate around its obstacles. Even immigrants who start out at the very bottom are making rapid gains, surging ahead of African-Americans and claiming the American dream for themselves. West Indians, for instance, have established a strong business and professional community, and have nearly achieved income parity with whites.[29]

How is this possible? The immigrants don't spend a lot of time contemplating the hardships of the past; their gaze is firmly fixed on the future. They recognize that education and entrepreneurship are the fastest ladders to success in America. They push their children to study, so that they will be admitted to Berkeley and MIT, and they pool their resources and set up small businesses, so that they can make some money and move to the suburbs. There are plenty of hurdles along the way, but the immigrant is sustained by the hope that he, or his children, will be able to break the chain of necessity and pursue the American dream.

Thus we find that any group that is trying to move up in America and succeed is confronted with two possible strategies—the immigrant strategy and the Jesse Jackson strategy—and it is an empirical question as to which one works better. So far the evidence is overwhelming that the immigrant approach of assimilating to the cultural strategies of success is vastly better for group uplift than the Jesse Jackson approach of political agitation.

One of the blessings of living in a multiracial society is that we can learn from one another. Black Americans have contributed greatly to America by pressuring the country to live up to its highest principles. As an immigrant, I owe a tremendous debt to the black civil rights movement for opening up doors that would otherwise have remained closed. All Americans have a lot to learn from African-Americans about suffering, about dignity, about creativity, and about charm. But it is also a fact that the black leadership can learn a lot from the immigrants, especially black immigrants. African-Americans can move up faster if they focus less on manufacturing representation and more on building intellectual and economic skills. In this way blacks can achieve a level of competitive success that is ultimately the best, and final, refutation of "rumors of inferiority."

Martin Luther King once said that ultimately every man must write with his own hand the charter of his emancipation proclamation. What he meant by this is that in a decent society, citizens will be granted equality of rights under the law. We do have that right, but we do not have any more rights than this. African-Americans were not always granted legal equality, but now they have it, and it is all that they are entitled to. King's point is that what we do with our rights, what we make of ourselves, the kind of script that we write of our lives, this finally is up to us.

CHAPTER FIVE

WHEN VIRTUE LOSES ALL HER LOVELINESS
Freedom and Its Abuses

> Hey! American man! You are a godless
> homosexual rapist of your grandmother's pet goat.
>
> —SALMAN RUSHDIE

T HE MOST SERIOUS CHARGE AGAINST AMERICA IS NOT that it is an oppressive society, or one that denies freedom and opportunity to minorities. It is the charge that America is an immoral society. Islamic fundamentalists hold that the United States and the West may be materially advanced but they are morally decadent. This is not a new perspective. Muslim travelers to the West have frequently commented on what they regard as the low state of Western morality, especially in the sexual domain. In one medieval Muslim account, a Frenchman comes home to find another man in bed with his wife:

"What brings you here to my wife?" he asks.

The man replies, "I was tired so I came in to rest."

"And how did you get into my bed?"

"I found the bed made, so I lay down on it."

"But the woman was sleeping with you!"

"It was her bed. Could I have kept her out of her own bed?"

"If you do this again," the Frenchman warns, "you and I will quarrel."[1]

The Muslim writer cites the incident to show the shocking moral laxity that he believes characterizes marriages in the West. If Muslims thought the level of Western sexual morality was bad in the Middle Ages, imagine what they must think of us today. Not surprisingly, Islamic criticisms of Western mores have intensified in modern times. As Sayyid Qutb observes, at least the West used to be Christian; now it is pagan. Qutb argues that modern America is suffering from *jahiliyya*—from the same polytheism, idolatry, and moral degeneracy that the prophet Muhammad found in the Bedouin tribes in the seventh century.

The Islamic view of Western immorality is supported by the observations of many critics within America and Europe. Vaclav Havel, president of the Czech Republic, recently termed the West "the first atheistic civilization in the history of humankind."[2] In 1978, in his famous Harvard address, the Soviet dissident Alexander Solzhenitsyn charged that in the West freedom has become another word for licentiousness, and "man's sense of responsibility to God and society has grown dimmer."[3] Many American conservatives and evangelical Christians share these concerns. Shortly after the September 11 terrorist attack, the editor of the evangelical weekly *World* described the World Trade Center as a modern Tower of Babel dedicated to the "false deities" of materialism, secularism, and relativism.[4] On the Right, figures such as Robert Bork, Bill Bennett, and Gary Bauer have warned that

American culture has deteriorated to the point that, in Bork's expression, the U.S. is "slouching towards Gomorrah."[5]

Some Americans will find this portrait of their country to be exaggerated and unduly harsh. They will point out, correctly, that many Americans are deeply religious, and that of all First World countries, America has the highest percentage of people who believe in God and go to church.[6] While recognizing that America exhibits a good deal of religious and moral diversity, these people note that this is the natural consequence of a society whose people come from different backgrounds and practice different faiths. They argue, too, that Hollywood movies and TV shows are entertainment—they should not be seen as representative of how people really live. The weirdos that we see on daytime talk shows, for instance, are the modern equivalent of circus freaks. Finally, we should note that in recent years crime and illegitimacy rates have declined, so that American culture is healthier in these respects.

While these are valid points, the criticisms of Qutb, Solzhenitsyn, Havel, Bork, and others cannot be so easily dismissed. True, Americans are probably more religious and socially conservative than Europeans, but that is not saying much, considering how decadent the Europeans are. Not withstanding all the picturesque churches that dot the American landscape, religion seems to have little or no public authority over society. And the "death of God" appears to have resulted, just as Nietzsche said it would, in the collapse of traditional morality and the rise of moral relativism. Even people who live upright, good lives have difficulty justifying their choices or regarding them as normative for others. Meanwhile, every depraved pervert—such as Rushdie's American character, who wants to have sex with a goat—can deflect criticism by invoking the relativist doctrine, "Who are you to impose your values on me?"

The disastrous consequences of this moral upheaval have been compiled by Bill Bennett in his *Index of Leading Cultural Indicators.*[7] But they are evident for all to see. America is a country where the traditional family seems to have irretrievably broken down: the typical marriage ends in divorce, and illegitimacy is now common across racial and socioeconomic lines. Behavior that is considered wrong and deviant in many cultures—such as premarital sex, homosexuality, and the use of pornography—is tolerated, if not accepted, in the United States. Newcomers are often shocked by the vulgarity and shamelessness of American popular culture that, even as entertainment, shapes the general tone of society. Perhaps one should not be surprised at the barbarism and weirdness of many American teenagers—their role models are people like Howard Stern, Dennis Rodman, Madonna, and the Artist Formerly Known as Prince.

Perhaps these anxieties about moral and cultural breakdown are mainly felt by conservatives, who tend to define morality narrowly in terms of what it is good to do (or, more precisely, not to do). But morality as classically understood also includes what it is good to be, and what it is good to love. This broader view of morality gives rise to a set of problems that is widely acknowledged throughout the culture. Thoughtful observers have noticed that Americans are extremely unsure of who they really are, what their highest priorities should be, and whether they are truly happy. Many people—not just young people but middle-aged guys like Newt Gingrich and Al Gore—go through identity crises in which they have to "find themselves." Life in the United States is characterized by a peculiar restlessness and angst, even in the midst of prosperity. Many Americans seek a higher sense of meaning or significance in their lives, yet it remains elusive, just over the horizon. Despite the gregariousness and affability of Americans, friendship and community appear to be scarce commodities in the United States. People are constantly in pursuit of love "relationships," yet few of these prove to be lasting. In most countries married life comes easily—its success is taken for granted—but in America married life is a struggle, and even happy marriages are haunted by the shadow of divorce.

All of this adds up to a powerful critique, which states that in America freedom has established itself as the highest value and has fatally undermined other cherished values. In other words, the triumph of freedom comes at the expense of decency, community, and virtue. Freedom in America means choice, and from the perspective of the critics, choice has been deified without regard to the content of choice. Consequently morality withers, and even choice itself ceases to matter because there is no significance to what one chooses. Good choices, bad choices: no one really cares. The result, in this view, is a debauched, demoralized, unhappy society. What is so great about American freedom if it leads to such deplorable results?

In this chapter I will argue that the critics who denounce the culture in this way are missing something vitally important about America. But we cannot deny that the problems they describe are real. What, then, is their cause? One answer, given

by many Islamic writers and some people in the U.S. as well, is
that the American system of technological capitalism is to blame.
Early in the twentieth century the economist Joseph Schumpeter
predicted that technological capitalism would produce massive
social upheaval. In Schumpeter's view, technological capitalism
unleashes a "gale of creative destruction" that undermines traditional institutions and traditional values.[8]

Clearly there is some truth to Schumpeter's analysis. Consider
the one thing that has done more to undermine morality in America than the combined influence of Darwin, Freud, Marx, and
Nietzsche. I speak, of course, of the automobile. Before the era of
the automobile most Americans lived on farms or in small towns.
Their virtue and chastity were sustained by the moral supervision
of the local community. A man looks out of his window. "Isn't
that Art Buckner's son? What's he up to? Hey! Stop that! Get out
of there!" What destroyed this comprehensive moral ecosystem
was the car. By providing universal access to the city, the car helped
to bring about the end of a whole way of life in America. The point
of this example is not to oppose cars, or to advocate that they be
outlawed, but to show that the apparatus of modern technology
makes inevitable some degree of moral change.

Technology has also helped to change women's roles and thus
to destabilize traditional "family values." Here the great catalyst
of social transformation was the mass movement of women into
the workplace. Feminists fought for women's right to have careers,
but their success was made possible by the pill, the vacuum cleaner,
and the forklift. Think about this: only a few decades ago, house-
work was a full-time occupation—cooking and cleaning took up
virtually the whole day. The vacuum cleaner and other domestic

appliances changed that. Until recently, work outside the home was harsh and physically demanding. Forklifts and other machines have reduced the need for human muscle. Finally, before the invention of the pill, women could not effectively control their reproduction, and therefore, for most women, the question of having a full-time career simply did not arise.

Like technology, capitalism has had a transforming effect on mores. Capitalism produces mass affluence, and mass affluence extends to ordinary people the same avenues of fulfillment—and of debauchery—previously available only to the upper class. Capitalism also produces a dynamic, mobile society in which people rarely end up living where they were born. Indeed, the average American moves a dozen times over the course of his life.[9] Only the "nuclear family" holds together; the extended family is scattered. Mobility also makes it difficult for Americans to form lasting friendships or to develop an enduring sense of community. Most relationships under capitalism are based on contract and mutual convenience. The commercial and social motto of America is: "Have a nice day." The pursuit of success under capitalism is also very time consuming and tends to shut out other demands on one's time. In Third World countries, if someone comes a long distance to see you, a month-long visit is considered insultingly short; in America, even relatives are expected to leave within a few days. While Americans treat others with respect and courtesy, they are not, in general, known for their hospitality.

The social traits I have here described are intrinsic to a free society oriented around technology and commerce. Important though they are, they are not the full story. To complete the story, we must examine the big change that came about in the 1960s, and was consolidated in the 1970s. You can see physical evidence of this change at the Yale Club in New York, where the photographs of Yale graduates are displayed. Through the 1950s and 1960s, these graduates present a neat, clean-cut appearance. Then, around 1969, the photographs tell a different story. The hair of the men gets longer, the hair of the women gets shorter. The hippie and the freak become recognizable social types. By the 1970s these changes have shaped virtually the whole class: the vast majority of graduates are seen sporting a languid, disheveled, rebel look. We can see a similar change by comparing the Beatles in the early 1960s with the Beatles in the early 1970s. By themselves these changes are merely cosmetic, but I am suggesting that they are outward manifestations of a much deeper alteration of outlook.

The 1960s and 1970s witnessed a moral revolution in the United States in which the idea of freedom was extended beyond anything the American founders envisioned. The change can be described in this way. The American founders believed that all people share a basic human nature, and therefore they want pretty much the same things in life. The founders set up a regime dedicated to three types of freedom—economic freedom, political freedom, and freedom of speech and religion—so that people could pursue happiness, or what we call the "American dream."

But this notion of freedom was radicalized in the 1960s. The change was brought about by the "counterculture," the mélange of antiwar activists, feminists, sexual revolutionaries, freedom riders, hippies, druggies, nudists, and vegetarians. Rebels they all were, and bohemians of one sort or another. The great thinker who stood behind them, the philosopher of bohemia, was Rousseau. This is not to say that Rousseau *caused* the social revolution. But he articulated its complaints and aspirations in the most eloquent, profound way. By examining Rousseau and what has been termed his "romantic" philosophy, we can more deeply understand the important moral shift that has occurred in America in the past few decades.

Rousseau was a deeply strange man. It has been said of him that he labored under the illusion that changes within his own life mirrored the great transformations of Western civilization. (Some have accused me of operating under the same delusion.) Many aspects of Rousseau's thought are misunderstood. Upon receiving a copy of Rousseau's *Discourse on the Origin of Inequality*, Voltaire wrote to him, "The desire to walk on all fours seizes one when one reads your work. Unfortunately I lost that habit more than 60 years ago."[10] Even today the popular impression is that Rousseau wanted us to abandon civilization and live the life of a noble savage. But Rousseau explicitly disclaims any such intention. "Although I want to form the man of nature," he writes, "the object is not to make him a savage and relegate him to the depths of the woods."[11] So, too, many people misunderstand Rousseau's concept of the "general will" as constituting some kind of an apologia for totalitarianism. In fact, Rousseau was a champion of radical freedom. We can see this by focusing on a central element of Rousseau's thought—the one that pertains to the "new morality" of the 1960s.

The philosopher Charles Taylor—whose interpretation of Rousseau I rely on throughout this chapter—expounds Rousseau's new idea: "There is a way of being human that is *my* way. I am called upon to live my life in this way, and not in imitation of anyone else's. If I do not, I miss the point of my life. I miss what being human is for *me*."[12] By insisting that each of us has an original way of being human, Rousseau is articulating the idea of individuality. But he is doing a lot more than that. Rousseau insists that in determining the unique course of one's life, the self is sovereign. To the American founders' list of freedoms, Rousseau adds a new one: inner freedom. In its most important manifestation, inner freedom is moral freedom—the freedom to determine what is good. But inner freedom also encompasses the broad range of choices that make one's life richer and more fulfilling. Rousseau argues that in deciding what to become, whom to marry, how to live, I should not go by the dictates of my parents, or my teachers, or my preachers, or even God. I should decide for myself alone.

How should I decide? By digging deep within myself. By consulting my inner compass, what Rousseau calls the "interior guide that never abandons us."[13] For Rousseau, we are beings with inner depths. The principles of truth, he writes, are "engraved in all hearts" and to discover what is right in a given situation, all we have to do is "commune with oneself."[14] As the Savoyard Vicar puts it in Rousseau's *Emile*, "I do not derive these rules from the principles of high philosophy, but I find them written by nature in ineffaceable characters at the bottom of my heart."[15] Here Rousseau is giving expression to the idea of authenticity, of being true to oneself.

It is a massively important idea. Before Rousseau, no one believed that each human life should follow its own distinctive moral course, nor did anyone think of giving the inner self—the voice of nature within us—final authority in determining that course. Rousseau's view emerged in resistance to an earlier view, according to which morality was a matter of costs and benefits. For Rousseau, calculation is the ethic of the *bourgeois,* the man of commerce. "Ancient politicians incessantly talked about morals and virtue," Rousseau writes. "Those of our time talk only of business and money."[16]

Rousseau's objection to the *bourgeois* is that he is a bit of a low character. His main goals are to improve his financial situation and move to a nicer neighborhood. The *bourgeois* wants to look good, smell clean, and have regular bowel movements. Medical checkups are a big thing with him; he wants to postpone death as long as possible. The *bourgeois* is far more concerned with his portfolio than with his soul. He spends all day doing corporate accounts or selling pest-control products, yet he is satisfied in his work. But how can one derive satisfaction from recording transactions all day, or from killing rats and cockroaches? The *bourgeois* is a man of limited horizons. However picayune his function, he is proud of his "work ethic." But as Oscar Wilde once noted, to have to do laborious work like sweeping floors and adding up numbers is depressing enough; to take *pride* in such things is absolutely appalling.

Rousseau's strongest complaint against the *bourgeois* is that he professes to be moral while acting like a mercenary. His virtues are entirely based on selfish calculation: he treats other people well in order to make a bigger profit. The *bourgeois* man doesn't care about being good; he only wants to appear good. His overriding concern is with his reputation. And in his social life, the *bourgeois* is obsessed with foolish vanity. Even his opinion of himself is derived from how he is perceived by others. His personality is so shaped by convention that he no longer knows who he really is. He is estranged from his own nature. He is a faker and a hypocrite. Even worse, he is not free because all his priorities and indeed his very identity are dependent on others. The conformity of the bourgeois is the mark of his unfreedom. Rousseau's charges are precisely the ones that the young people of the 1960s launched against their parents.

Against the false values of the *bourgeois*—against his artificiality and hypocrisy—Rousseau offered the alternative of primitive man, natural man, of Homo sapiens before the advent of civilization. Rousseau admits that natural man may never have really existed: he is a kind of mental construct, a "hypothesis." Nevertheless, Rousseau finds it very illuminating to imagine what such a man might be like. He would be a savage, yes, but a noble savage. His selfishness would be confined to meeting his immediate bodily needs. Confronted by suffering on the part of his fellows, natural man would feel pity. Natural man is not virtuous—he doesn't even know what that is—but he does have a basic innocence and goodness. Natural man is without vanity or pretense, the evils that Rousseau believes have been introduced by "civilization." Rousseau also admires natural man because he is free: he has no prescribed duties, obeys no one, and follows no law other than his own will.

Still, Rousseau is under no illusion that modern people can recover natural man. Having been imbued with civilization, we cannot now return to the forest and live with the bears. But if a return to nature is impossible, Rousseau argues that there is a second option available to us. We can recover the voice of nature in us. If man's original home cannot be restored as a place, it can be restored as a state of mind. Charles Taylor terms this "self-determining freedom." In Taylor's words, "I am free when I decide for myself what concerns me, rather than being shaped by external influences. Our moral salvation comes from recovering authentic moral contact with ourselves. Self-determining freedom demands that I break the hold of external impositions, and decide for myself alone."[17]

It is only when the layers of artificiality and convention are removed that one's true self emerges. For Rousseau, the true self is characterized by originality, sincerity, and compassion. He makes virtues out of all three. In his *Confessions* Rousseau writes, "I am not made like any of those I have seen; I venture to believe that I am not made like any of those who are in existence."[18] Rousseau proves the point by giving us an autobiography like none that was written before him. Commenting on Rousseau's revelations, Irving Babbit writes, "Never has a man of such undoubted genius shown himself so lacking in humility and decency."[19] Rousseau raises the curtain on all kinds of forbidden experiences, including masturbation, adultery, voyeurism, visits to brothels, even incest and sadomasochism. Far from being embarrassed about discussing such topics, Rousseau revels in them.

Yet there is nothing cheap or sordid about Rousseau. He deals with intimate experiences with such passion, tenderness, and seriousness that the overall effect is to heighten our fascination. Generations of critics have denounced Rousseau as self-indulgent, disgusting, and perverted. They have noted that he fathered several children out of wedlock and then abandoned them to an orphanage; Rousseau can be seen as the original deadbeat dad.

But none of these criticisms has diminished Rousseau's appeal. Rousseau's answer to them is something like the following: If I am not worth as much as you are, at least I am different. I may not be as virtuous, but I am my own person. You may not like my self-description, but you have to credit me with giving an honest account of myself. You may find me unappealing, but at least I am sincere. Finally, if I have not lived an irreproachable life, I am a well-meaning and good person, and I care. The reader may recognize in this portrait the moral code of a certain American ex-president.

To understand why Rousseau's ideas are so controversial, to see why their consolidation in the 1960s and 1970s continues to torment and divide Americans, it is helpful to contrast Rousseau's *Confessions* with another book of the same title: the *Confessions* of St. Augustine. Augustine, of course, was one of the early church fathers, and at first glance his account of morality seems to be quite similar to that of Rousseau. "I entered into the depths of my soul," Augustine writes, "and with the eye of my soul I saw the Light that never changes casting its rays over me."[20] In Augustine's view, God is not to be found "out there" but within our hearts. God is the interior light that powers our souls.

Both Augustine and Rousseau counsel inwardness as the means to truth. Rousseau's innovation is to cut off this quest from any external source of authority, including that of God. For Rousseau the self *defines* what is good; the inner light is the final arbiter of how I should live my life. Augustine, by contrast, presumed that the inward journey is merely the pathway to the Creator. The inner light is controlled by an outer source, and that is God. Another way to put it is that Augustine presumes that there is a moral order in the universe that is separate from us and that makes claims on us. The existence of such an order was taken for granted by virtually all the great thinkers of the ancient world— Christian and non-Christian, Western and non-Western, believers as well as atheists.[21] Its laws were considered no less valid than, say, the laws governing the motion of the tides and the planets.

In America, of course, the moral order was represented by Christianity. Intellectuals have been rebelling against the Christian order for several centuries. But I think it is fair to say that until the 1950s—the era of the "greatest generation"—the Christian paradigm held firm in America. It had been modified over time to take into account the multiplicity of Christian denominations, as well as the presence of Jews—hence the attempt at forging a Judeo-Christian synthesis. Despite these accommodations, the vast majority of Americans in the 1950s believed that, for human beings in general, there was a "right way" to live and a "wrong way" to live, and they were pretty confident that they knew the difference between the two. There was a whole moral framework that this group took for granted.

What changed in the 1960s in America is the collapse of this framework, the erosion of belief in this external order. For the first time many people, especially young people, began to find the external rules arbitrary, senseless, and oppressive. The counterculture did not reject morality; it was passionately concerned with morality. But it substituted Rousseau's conception of the inner compass for the old rules of obligation. Getting in touch

with one's feelings and being true to oneself were now more important than conforming to the preexisting moral consensus of society. By embracing the new morality, the children of the 1960s
became incomprehensible to their parents. And as this new generation inherited the reins of power, its ethos entered the mainstream. As a consequence of this change, America became a
different country.

The magnitude of the change is evident when we consider the
philosophical presuppositions of the "old morality" and the "new
morality." The old morality was based on the premise that human
nature is flawed. Since human beings are inclined to do bad things,
consulting the inner self becomes a very misguided thing to do.
The self is the enemy; the self is under the sway of the passions;
the self must be overcome. The wayward passions must be ruled
by the mind or brought to submission by the will. Through reason or revelation, human beings acquire knowledge of the external order. Conformity to that order is the measure of how good
a person you are. And the institutions of society should be devised
in such a way as to steer flawed or sinful human beings away from
temptation and to keep them on the straight path.

Rousseau turns this paradigm upside down. For him, human
nature is basically good. It is society that corrupts man. The means
of this corruption is reason, which is deployed to enable one man
to advance above another, to accumulate more than the other, to
appear good in the eyes of everybody. Since reason has become
an instrument of sordid calculation, it is the enemy of morality
and truth. In order to discover what is good and true, we must
set aside reason and be in touch with our feelings. This is the
romantic element in Rousseau. According to him, feelings never

lie because they speak with the voice of nature itself. By listening to that inner voice, and following it, we can rise above the corruptions and compromises that society seeks from us, and we can recover our natural goodness.

The triumph of Rousseau's worldview gives rise to a new set of problems that could not have arisen under the old order. In earlier eras people didn't have "identity crises" because their moral identity was supplied by the ethical framework that they all took for granted. This ethical framework might emphasize different virtues in different times or places—thus one society emphasizes the warrior ethic, another the ascetic life, a third the life of production and the family. The challenge that people faced was one of living up to the moral order. The Spartan soldier might have wondered whether he was courageous enough not to retreat in the face of certain death. The medieval Christian monk might have doubted his ability to live by the Benedictine Rule. Undoubtedly there were members of the "greatest generation" who struggled to conform to the demands imposed on them by the regnant code: to remain faithful to their wives, go to church on Sunday, show up for battle when drafted, and so on. But in each case some external framework remained in place and provided an unquestioned standard by which human action was judged.

In Rousseau's new world, however, the external framework ceases to be authoritative for the whole society. A person can, of course, join the marines and embrace the military code, or become a Muslim and follow the Islamic regimen. But now it is the individual's act of choosing that is important. No one sees it as *obvious* that the military life or the Islamic life is the best or highest calling. Most people's reaction is, "Well, if it works for you," and

"Well, if you're happy." In other words, each person must select his or her priorities and moral commitments in a society where other people are sure to choose differently, and in which there are obvious trade-offs to be made.

In Rousseau's world, moral identity is a problem because it is not given: it is self-generated. Authenticity and self-fulfillment represent an ongoing pursuit, and there is constant anxiety from the knowledge that this pursuit can fail. A person who feels inwardly directed to be an artist might, for various reasons, take a job in banking and spend the rest of his life feeling that he has betrayed his true calling, that he has "sold out." Moreover, even commitments that are satisfying at a given time can lose their hold on us; when this happens to the whole moral outlook we have chosen, the result is utter confusion, a crisis of identity. An "identity crisis" is what happens to you when a set of commitments that once seemed right no longer makes sense to you: suddenly you are cut adrift, you have lost your horizon, you no longer know who you are.[22] These problems are peculiar to a society that has adopted the ethic of authenticity: in other words, they are American problems.

The principles of Rousseau did not make their first appearance in the 1960s. One hears strong echoes of them in Emerson's ethic of self-reliance, and in Thoreau's quest for inner harmony through solitude. Rousseau is the guiding spirit of bohemia, and early in the twentieth century one could find bohemia on the Left Bank in Paris or in Greenwich Village in New

York. But the bohemian spirit was confined to intellectual and artistic enclaves. It defined itself against the prevailing norms of society, which were mainly bourgeois and Christian. What changed in the late 1960s and 1970s is that the bohemian culture became part of the mainstream culture. It is not the only culture: One can still find, especially in the heartland, recalcitrant remnants of the old culture. Orthodox Jews, Catholics, and Protestants continue to affirm the existence of an independent moral hierarchy. But the bohemian culture now sets the tone for the society at large, and it commands a strong allegiance among the young.

Why did the ethic of authenticity win such widespread acceptance in America? Because the drive that sustained the generation of the 1930s and 1940s could no longer sustain its children. The people in the "greatest generation" worked hard to triumph over scarcity and to win the freedom to make their own life—exactly what powers immigrants to the United States today. For those who grew up during the Great Depression, the conquest of necessity was a moral imperative—to own a house, to put food on the table, to save for the children's college education—and when they succeeded in this they felt a profound sense of achievement and satisfaction.

But their children found themselves in a different situation. They took comfort and security and opportunity for granted, and sought something more—something to give uniqueness and significance to their lives. In this quest, they often viewed the dogmatic rules, social conformity, and materialistic preoccupations of their parents as soulless and alienating. At this point they became prime candidates for conversion to Rousseau's way of thinking. He offered them a way to find originality and moral purpose, yet in a way that did not compromise their freedom. The success of Rousseau reflects a failure on the part of the "greatest generation": it failed to replicate itself. The children of the World War II generation emphatically and often bitterly repudiated the moral code of their parents. They rebelled by defecting to Rousseau's camp.

Today we can see the triumph of authenticity in the enormous importance that American society grants to the "artist." I use the term to cover not just painters but also writers, sculptors, actors, musicians, even athletes. In our time a large number of Americans aspire to be artists. I can't tell you how many orthodontists, venture capitalists, housewives, and limousine drivers have greeted me with the sentence, "I too am writing a book." I sometimes find this annoying: when I meet a cardiologist at a cocktail party, I don't say, "I too am thinking about doing heart transplants."

But I cannot blame the aspiring authors: being an artist is cool. And rich people who cannot be artists frequently try to identify with artists in some way. Tom Wolfe has pointed out that in America today it is much more fashionable to donate a million dollars to the Metropolitan Museum of Art than to give it to the Presbyterian Church. The CEO's wife would much rather sit on the museum board than on the parish committee. Indeed, it is no exaggeration to say that art has replaced religion as the leading cultural institution in America.

The reason that we admire artists is that they draw upon resources within themselves to express something that is distinctively their own. Think of such American originals as Ernest Hemingway, Elvis Presley, Allen Ginsberg, Muhammad Ali, Jack Nicholson, and Oprah Winfrey. It is hard to see these people bearing a close resemblance to their parents. They seem to have sprung out of their own self-conception; they have created their own public identities. We cherish them as pure originals. Historically, of course, art was not seen as producing anything new or unique; indeed, the artist was viewed as an imitator—one who makes copies of nature. The Greeks had a story about an artist who was so skilled that when he painted grapes the birds would peck at them. But today art is not admired for its fidelity to nature but for its fidelity to "inner nature." Contemporary art is seen as a vehicle for self-discovery and self-expression.

Our society attaches great prestige to this quest for authenticity, even when it takes strange or controversial forms. For instance, who can deny that there is something bizarre and even repulsive about people like Dennis Rodman, Howard Stern, Madonna, and Prince? At the same time, most Americans find them fascinating. There is something vibrant, creative, and distinctive about them; they live their lives in italics. Moreover, their outrageousness marks them as nonconformists who refuse to change their ways in order to satisfy social convention. Their personality says to the world, "Whether you like it or not, this is the way I am." Americans recognize the voice of authenticity here, and this is why they are so tolerant of such extremities. Indeed, the United States gives more latitude than any other society to the claims of the loner, the dissenter, and the eccentric. In other countries these people are viewed as losers, malcontents, or crackpots. In America, however, they are seen as undaunted souls who are following their inner convictions even at the cost of social rejection.

It is practically a definition of the cultural mainstream to say that the idea of authenticity—of being "true to oneself"—is now

the new morality. We see it in corporate advertising: "Just Do It."
"Think Different." "The Greatest Risk Is Not Taking One."
Rousseau's influence is also evident in the rise of "victimhood"
and "compassion" as political principles. As Clifford Orwin and
Nathan Tarcov write, "It was Rousseau who taught us to think
of ourselves as good and to blame our sufferings and crimes on
society."[23] As for the politics of compassion, Democrats have been
displaying moist eyes in public for at least three decades, but now
even the Bush administration proclaims its allegiance to "com-
passionate conservatism."

Authenticity is also the guiding force behind what Arthur
Melzer has termed "the modern cult of sincerity." As Melzer puts
it, "I must 'be myself' regardless of *what* I might be." This trait
reveals itself in the tendency to confess one's sins in public. From
former drug addicts giving church testimonies, to reformed Nazis
telling all to Montel Williams, to politicians holding press con-
ferences to acknowledge their indiscretions, Americans are a self-
revealing lot. Indeed, the worse the confession, the more eagerly
it is promulgated and the more enthusiastically it is received.
Melzer dryly observes, "Heroes of sincerity are to be found only
among the most unfortunate or depraved."[24]

Today even the traditional enemies of authenticity shape their
lifestyles according to its code. Successful entrepreneurs and exec-
utives sometimes opt out of their businesses when they find the
work "unfulfilling." It is now common practice for vice presidents
and sales managers of companies to go mountain climbing in the
Rockies, or in Tibet, to "find themselves." Even the *bourgeoisie*
now concede the validity of Rousseau's moral critique and seek to
live by his precepts. And the staid U.S. Supreme Court a few years
ago endorsed the ethic of authenticity when it declared that all

Americans have a "right to define one's own concept of existence, of meaning, of the universe, and of the mystery of human life."[25]

Whenever there is a battle in the popular culture between the old values and the new ethic of authenticity, authenticity usually wins. Recently I was watching one of the daytime talk shows on television. The guests on the show were a married couple, but with a difference: both partners had had sex change operations. The man had become a woman, and the woman had become a man. The premise of the show was that their sex life was better than ever! No sooner did the couple advance this thesis than an elderly lady in the audience stood up and chided them: "What you people are doing is sick, sick, sick." And there was a spattering of applause on behalf of this normal human reaction. But interestingly this is not the point of view that prevailed. As the show went on, the guests made their appeal to the ethic of authenticity. "This lifestyle may seem bizarre *to you*," they said, "but it works *for us*." "This is something that we felt we had to do, and so we went for it." "We're happy, so what's your problem with it?" "Who are you to impose *your* morality on us?" And by the end of the show the audience was cheering this position.

Although I am an immigrant, I feel the power of the ideal of authenticity. Several years ago I invoked it in a conversation I had with my father, in which I was trying to convince him to support my decision to become a writer. His instinctive reaction was that writing was a fine hobby, but not something that a serious person should undertake as a career. He felt about writing what I feel about chess: it's too serious to be a game, but not serious enough to be an occupation. "Get your MBA," my dad advised, "and then maybe you can do something useful with your life." I tried to explain that I felt called to be a writer and that I wanted a life that made me feel true to myself. "What you are saying," my father said, "is that there is a little being that lives inside of you. Let's call him Little Dinesh. Little Dinesh apparently has the wisdom and authority to run your life. And apparently you communicate and converse with Little Dinesh. You worry that you have lost touch with him, and you are eager to renew contact. You feel that becoming a writer will allow you to stay on intimate terms with Little Dinesh." My point isn't that my father *disagreed* with me; he didn't know what the heck I was talking about.

The ideal of authenticity now helps to define what it means to be an American; beyond our shores many people find it incredible and incomprehensible. Even within the United States it is controversial: many cultural conservatives react to it with fear and loathing. Irving Babbit's famous critique of Rousseau anticipates many of the charges we hear today. Babbit sees Rousseau as simply weird, exhibiting "an eccentricity so extreme as to be almost or quite indistinguishable from madness." The ethic of authenticity, Babbit writes, undermines the Christian notions of sin and individual self-restraint. Self-fulfillment is, in Babbit's view, another term for selfishness. Babbit alleges that Rousseau is an advocate of a new form of immorality that is all the more dangerous because it is presented in esthetically allur- ing garb.[26] Babbit's indictment has been echoed in recent years by cultural conservatives such as Allan Bloom, Patrick Buchanan, Bill Bennett, and Robert Bork. These men would like nothing better than to uproot the ethic of authenticity and restore the moral consensus that existed in the 1950s.

The problems with this root-and-branch repudiation of contemporary ideals can be seen by considering an example, which I offer as representative of the whole culture of authenticity. Recently I stopped into my neighborhood Starbucks, and there, behind the counter, was a specimen who probably would not have existed in earlier generations. I surveyed him with curious fascination: the Mohawk hair, the earrings, the nose ring, the studs on his forehead and tongue, the tattoos. I could just imagine Judge Bork entering the room. His immediate reaction would probably be, "Arrest that man." Since this is not practical, another option would be to grab the young fellow and yell, "What is wrong with you, you demented freak!" From Bork's point of view there is simply no excuse for some people.

But what good would come of this? The epithets and remonstrations of the conservative have no chance of persuading the Starbucks guy. Indeed, they are likely to have the opposite effect: "Get away from me, you fascist!" From the Starbucks guy's perspective, the cultural conservatives are enemies of freedom. He would undoubtedly regard Judge Bork as a self-righteous mullah who is trying to tell him how to live his life. The Starbucks guy believes that he has the inalienable right to determine his own destiny, to make his own choices. Thus he regards the conservative approach as presumptuous, coercive, and un-American. And he is reluctant to listen to anything these conservatives have to say.

The Starbucks guy's objection to the conservatives is valid on two counts. First, many conservatives do sound like they are against freedom. Bork, for example, has urged the enforcement of "public morality" through the censorship of objectionable songs, movies, TV shows, and Internet websites.[27] Buchanan heartily agrees, calling state censorship "an idea whose time has come."[28] Some religious and political activists have gone further, demanding laws that enforce Christian precepts or the norms that prevailed in the 1950s. I cannot see how such strategies could possibly work. Is it realistic for a democratic society to enforce norms based on a moral order that is no longer shared by the community? How can a political strategy that defines itself against America's core value of freedom possibly succeed? Cultural conservatives must recognize that the new morality is now entrenched and pervasive, so that there is no way to go back to the shared moral hierarchy of the past, however fondly that era may live on in their memories.

Second, the root-and-branch rejection of authenticity ignores the moral force of this ideal. Contrary to what the cultural conservatives fear, the new morality is not simply a screen for self-indulgence and immorality. If you were to sympathetically engage the Starbucks guy in conversation and ask him to account for himself, he would probably say, "I am trying to be unique." "I want to be an individual." "I am trying to be me." Some may find these aspirations banal, even comical, but the goals for which the Starbucks guy is striving are legitimate ones. Even at the cost of bodily pain, he wants a distinctive identity, a life that is not simply a copy of other people's lives. In short, he wants a life that counts.

I do not think that it is either right or prudent to attack him for this. The Starbucks guy is an idealist, and it would be wrong to trample on that idealism. Moreover, his ethic of authenticity is entrenched in his psyche; how realistic would it be to uproot it? A much better approach for conservatives is to acknowledge the legitimacy of the ideal of authenticity, but to make the case that the Starbucks guy has adopted a debased form of it. The Starbucks guy wants to be original, and this is a good thing to be, but it may be pointed out to him that he is not succeeding in this, because every fourth guy at Starbucks looks like him! Perhaps there are more meaningful ways for the Starbucks guy to convey his individuality: through art, for example, or by dedicating himself to a cause he believes in.

Instead of completely denying the value of expressive freedom, conservatives would do better to embrace it—at least in part—and to focus on educating people about the rich moral sources of freedom, and about how to use freedom well. But the conservative is not the only one who needs to change; the Starbucks guy does too. He needs to realize that his bold stance against the institutions of society—against commerce, against family, against community, against morality—is a bit of a pose. Indeed, it fails by its own standard: it is inauthentic. After all, it is our rich, commercial society that makes an establishment like Starbucks viable. It is the legal, social, and moral norms of the community that provide the guardrails protecting the Starbucks guy's freedom and autonomy. Moreover, it is the hard work, discipline, deferred gratification, and frugality of his parents over the years that now enable the Starbucks guy to enjoy his bohemian lifestyle. True, the Starbucks guy is in a situation different from his parents', but they are the ones who have placed him there. In short, a little gratitude and understanding should not be too much to expect from the Starbucks guy.

In addition, champions of authenticity and moral autonomy like the Starbucks guy should understand that identity is not completely self-generated and that freedom is not its own justification. Our identity and self-image emerge out of our relationships with others. Even the Starbucks guy's studs and tattoos are an attempt to communicate *something* to *somebody*. Ultimately this expressive freedom must have some underlying purpose. Freedom becomes insignificant if it makes no difference what I choose. Thus the Starbucks guy's mantra "I can choose for myself" raises the next and indispensable question, "What are you going to choose?" It is not enough to answer, "Whatever my inner self dictates." Even the inner self needs a compass—it operates according to some substantive understanding of the good life. There is no cause to believe that this understanding is impervious to reason and cannot be shaped through education and discussion. The grave weakness of the ethic of authenticity is that it evades this fundamental issue and simply stresses the autonomy of choice.

Since the earliest days of Athens and Jerusalem, most of the great figures of Western civilization have regarded the question of the content of the good life as the central one. The American founders agreed with this, and they created a mechanism that allows people to pursue the good life without government interference. Since the triumph of authenticity in the 1960s and 1970s, the emphasis has been on radical freedom, largely to the exclusion of the question of what that freedom is for. The great conservative challenge is to bring this issue back to the forefront. Our freedom and autonomy are precious commodities, and conservatives better than anyone else recognize that it is a great tragedy when they are trivialized and abused. Their mission, therefore, is to steer the American ethic of authenticity to its highest manifestation and to ennoble freedom by showing it the path to virtue.

CHAPTER SIX

AMERICA
THE BEAUTIFUL
What We're Fighting For

We have it in our power to begin the world
all over again.

—THOMAS PAINE

AMERICA REPRESENTS A NEW WAY OF BEING HUMAN AND
thus presents a radical challenge to the world. On the
one hand, Americans have throughout their history held
that they are special: that their country has been blessed by God,
that the American system is unique, that Americans are not like
people everywhere else. This set of beliefs is called "American
exceptionalism." At the same time, Americans have also traditionally insisted that they provide a model for the world, that theirs
is a formula that others can follow, and that there is no better life
available elsewhere. Paradoxically enough, American exceptionalism leads to American universalism.

Both American exceptionalism and American universalism
have come under fierce attack from the enemies of America, both

161

at home and abroad. The critics of America deny that there is anything unique about America, and they ridicule the notion that the American model is one that others should seek to follow. Indeed, by chronicling the past and present crimes of America, they hope to extract apologies and financial reparations out of Americans. Some even seek to justify murderous attacks against America on the grounds that what America does, and what she stands for, invites such attacks.

These critics are aiming their assault on America's greatest weakness: her lack of moral self-confidence. Americans cannot effectively fight a war without believing that it is a just war. That's why America has only lost once, in Vietnam, and that was because most Americans did not know what they were fighting for. The enemies of America understand this vulnerability. At the deepest level their assault is moral: they seek to destroy America's belief in herself, knowing that if this happens, America is finished. By the same token, when Americans rally behind a good cause, as in World War II, they are invincible. The outcome of America's engagements abroad is usually determined by a single factor: America's will to prevail. In order to win, Americans need to believe that they are on the side of the angels. The good news is that they usually are.

America's enemies are likely to respond to these assertions with sputtering outrage. Their view is that America's influence has been, and continues to be, deeply destructive and wicked. As we have seen, this criticism comes from different directions: from multiculturalists who allege historical racism and the ongoing oppression of minorities; from Third World intellectuals who deplore the legacy of colonialism; from Western leftists who see America as a force for evil in the world; and from Islamic fundamentalists and cultural conservatives who view America as culturally decadent and morally degenerate.

These attacks on America usually begin with complaints about America's foreign policy. Many European, Islamic, and Third World critics—as well as many American leftists—make the point that the United States uses the comforting language of morality while operating according to the ruthless norms of power politics. This is a theme that we in America hear endlessly from leftist intellectuals like Edward Said, Noam Chomsky, and Michael Lerner; it is a also a theme that Muslim fundamentalists have stressed. To these critics, America is guilty of such foreign policy outrages as overthrowing democratically elected regimes in Iran and Chile; propping up dictatorships in Latin America and now in the Middle East; fighting to protect oil fields in the Gulf War while pretending to be fighting for the rights of Kuwaitis; ignoring massive human rights violations where no American interests are involved; starving hundreds of thousands of Iraqi children through a cruel policy of economic sanctions; and demonizing people like Saddam Hussein and Osama bin Laden whom the United States itself once supported.

These are serious charges, and they seek to expose as wide a chasm between American ideals and American actions as there was between the rhetoric of Pericles' funeral oration and Athens's ruthless massacre of the citizens of the island of Melos. While Pericles sang lofty hymns to freedom, the Athenian ambassadors conveyed a different message in the Melian dialogue: if you do not submit to slavery, they told the Melians, we will destroy you, and our reason for doing so is because we can, because the law of nature dictates that "the strong do what they have the power to do and the weak accept what they have to accept."[1] In short, the Athenian ambassadors made explicit the law of *realpolitik*: that nations act based not on ideals but on their interests, and that in the field of international affairs, might inevitably makes right.

In his book *White House Years,* Henry Kissinger says essentially the same thing about American foreign policy: America has no permanent friends or enemies, only interests.[2] And in a sense this is true: The American people have empowered their government to act on their behalf against adversaries. They have not asked their government to be neutral between their interests and, say, the interests of the Ethiopians. It is unreasonable to ask a nation to ignore its interests, because that is tantamount to asking a nation to ignore the welfare of its people. Everywhere in the world this is taken for granted. Asked recently why he once supported the Taliban regime and then joined the American effort to oust it, General Pervez Musharaff of Pakistan coolly replied, "Because our national interest has changed." When he said this, nobody thought to ask any further questions.

Critics of United States foreign policy judge it by a standard that they apply to no one else. They denounce America for promoting its self-interest while expecting other countries to protect their self-interest. Americans do not need to apologize for the fact that their country acts abroad in a way that is good for them. Why should it act in any other way? Indeed, Americans can feel immensely proud about how often their country has served them well while simultaneously promoting noble ideals and the welfare of others. So yes, America did fight the Gulf War *in part* to protect its access to oil, but it *also* fought to liberate Kuwait from Iraqi invasion. American interests did not taint American ideals; indeed, the opposite is true: the ideals dignified the interests.

But what about U.S. backing for Latin American, Asian, and Middle Eastern dictators, such as Somoza in Nicaragua, Marcos in the Philippines, Pinochet in Chile, and the shah of Iran? It should be noted that, in each of these cases, the United States eventually turned against the dictatorial regime and actively aided in its ouster. In Chile and the Philippines, the results were favorable: the Pinochet and Marcos regimes were replaced by democratic governments that have so far endured. In Nicaragua and Iran, however, one form of tyranny promptly gave way to another. Somoza was replaced by the Sandinistas, who suspended civil liberties and established a Marxist-style dictatorship, and the shah of Iran was replaced by a harsh theocracy presided over by the Ayatollah Khomeini.

These outcomes help to highlight a crucial principle of foreign policy: the principle of the lesser evil. This means that one should not pursue a thing that seems good if it is likely to result in something worse. A second implication of this doctrine is that one is usually justified in allying with a bad guy in order to oppose a regime that is even more terrible. The classic example of this occurred in World War II. The United States allied with a very bad man—Stalin—in order to defeat someone who was even worse and posed a greater threat at the time—Hitler. Once the principle of the lesser evil is taken into account, then many American actions in terms of toppling socialist and anti-Western forces, and also of backing Third World dictators like Marcos and Pinochet, become defensible. These were measures taken to fight the Cold War. If one accepts what is today an almost universal consensus—that the Soviet Union was an "evil empire"—then the U.S. was right to attach more importance to the fact that Marcos and Pinochet were reliably anti-Soviet than to the fact that they were autocratic thugs.

A second principle crucial in understanding foreign policy is that of situational logic. Situations change, and therefore policies must be devised to deal with a particular situation at a given time. It is foolish to hold the U.S. culpable for "inconsistently" changing its policy when the underlying situation that justified the original policy has also changed. By this reasoning, there was nothing wrong with America supporting Saddam Hussein in the late 1970s and early 1980s, when the greatest threat in the region came from Iran; so, too, America was justified during the 1980s in providing weapons to the mujahideen, even if this group included Osama bin Laden, in order to drive the Soviet Union out of Afghanistan. Obviously when the Cold War ended and, under new circumstances, Hussein and bin Laden emerged as the greatest threats, America shifted its focus and began to treat them more severely. Let us also remember that we know things today about Hussein and bin Laden that were not known then. We cannot fault American policymakers in the 1970s and early 1980s for not possessing knowledge about Hussein and bin Laden that only became available in the 1990s.

What, then, of the starvation of the Iraqi children? This has become a staple complaint of American leftists, and it is one that bin Laden has repeatedly raised. The fallacy of this argument is contained in its premise: that by refusing to trade with Iraq America is to blame that Iraqi children are hungry. To see this fallacy, consider an example. I am walking down the street, eating a sandwich. You approach me, give me an account of your troubles, and ask me to share my sandwich with you. For whatever reason, I decline to do so. Now my reasons for this refusal may be good ones or bad ones. But in either case I am not to blame for your plight. I didn't *cause* your hunger. So, too, one can agree or disagree with America's policy of sanctions, but America is not responsible for the fact that Iraqi children are starving. The reason they are starving is that they are under the subjugation of a barbarous dictator who spends Iraq's oil revenues on his own indulgences and doesn't seem to care whether Iraqi children live or die.

None of this is to excuse the blunders and mistakes that have characterized U.S. foreign policy over the decades. Unlike the old colonial powers—the British and the French—the Americans seem to have little aptitude for the nuances of international politics. Part of the problem is America's astonishing ignorance of the rest of the world. About this the detractors of the United States are right. The critics have also played a constructive role in exposing America's misdoings. Here each person can develop his own list: long-standing U.S. support for a Latin despot, or the unjust internment of the Japanese in World War II, or America's reluctance to impose sanctions on South Africa's apartheid regime. There is ongoing debate over whether the U.S. was right to drop atomic bombs on Hiroshima and Nagasaki.

However one feels about these cases, let us concede to the critics the point that America is not always in the right. What the critics completely ignore, however, is the other side of the ledger. Twice in the twentieth century, the United States saved the world: first from the Nazi threat, then from Soviet totalitarianism. After destroying Germany and Japan in World War II, America proceeded to rebuild both nations, and today they are close allies. Now the U.S. is helping Afghanistan on the path to political stability and economic development. (What this tells us is that North Vietnam's misfortune was to *win* the war against the U.S. If it had lost, it wouldn't be the impoverished country it is now, because America would have rebuilt and modernized it.) Consider, too, how magnanimous the United States has been to the former Soviet Union after victory in the Cold War. And even though the United States does not have a serious military rival in the world today, America has not acted in the manner of regimes that have historically occupied this enviable position. For the most part, America is an *abstaining* superpower: it shows no real interest in conquering and subjugating the rest of the world. (Imagine how the Soviets would have acted if they had won the Cold War.) On occasion the U.S. intervenes to overthrow a tyrannical regime or to halt massive human rights abuses in another country, but it never stays to rule that country. In Grenada and Haiti and Bosnia, the United States got in and then it got out. Moreover, when America does get into a war, it is supremely careful to avoid targeting civilians and to minimize collateral damage. During the military campaign against the Taliban, U.S. defense secretary Donald Rumsfeld met with theologians to make sure that America's actions were in strict conformity with "just war" principles.[3] And even as America bombed the Taliban's infrastructure and hideouts, its planes dropped rations of food to avert hardship and starvation of Afghan civilians. What other country does these things?

Jeane Kirkpatrick once said, "Americans need to face the truth about themselves, no matter how pleasant it is." The reason that many Americans don't feel this way is that they judge themselves by a higher standard than anyone else. Americans are a self-scrutinizing people: even if they have acted well in a given situation, they are always ready to examine whether they could have acted better. At some subliminal level, everybody knows this. Thus if the Chinese, the Arabs, or the sub-Saharan Africans slaughter ten thousand of their own people, the world utters a collective sigh and resumes its normal business. We sadly expect the Chinese, the Arabs, and the sub-Saharan Africans to do these things. By contrast, if America, in the middle of a war, accidentally bombs a school or a hospital and kills two hundred civilians, there is an immediate uproar and an investigation is launched. What all this demonstrates, of course, is America's evident moral superiority.

The moral superiority of America is vehemently denied in three camps: among leftist intellectuals, especially in Europe and the Third World; among American multiculturalists; and among Islamic fundamentalists. These three groups make up the "blame America first" crowd. The discontent of the intellectuals seems to originate mostly from peevishness and envy. The Europeans are haunted by the knowledge that they once had an empire and directed the course of world affairs; now they play the part of assistant coach on America's team. This subservient role is very annoying, especially given the high opinion that most European intellectuals have of themselves.

For Third World intellectuals, it is simply unbearable to acknowledge how good America is because then they are forced to admit how bad their own countries are. After one of my lectures, a graduate student from Sri Lanka came up to me and protested, "I cannot agree with what you are saying, because if you are right, then I don't know what to say to people in my country. Am I supposed to tell my people that America is the best and that they are *shit?*" I didn't know quite what to say, so I replied, "Well, I'm not sure I would put it *that way.*" But I was struck by the degree of his agitation. My numerous conversations with Third World savants convince me that they are disgraced by American greatness, and their anti-Americanism is a way to salvage pride.

Multiculturalists have a different reason for objecting to American superiority. In their view, the United States cannot be morally superior because no culture is morally superior to any other culture. The multiculturalists hold that there are no universal standards by which cultures can be judged better or worse. All cultures are basically equal. This, of course, is the multicultural doctrine of cultural relativism. This doctrine was first articulated in the early part of the twentieth century and has been adopted by multiculturalists in the past few decades. Multiculturalists are committed to cultural relativism in large part because they see it as a weapon against racism. Racists are prevented from asserting the superiority of their culture because the very concept of superiority is denied at the outset. Cultural relativism also appeals to American intellectuals in general because they don't like approaching other societies with the assumption that their own way is always better. The presumption of cultural equality strikes them as a much fairer and more reasonable way to study other cultures.

As a methodological starting point, the premise of cultural relativism seems unobjectionable. Before we know anything about the Papuans, we might fully expect that they have their Proust and Einstein. In examining that culture we should of course be very careful to allow for various forms of knowledge and discovery: their Proust may not closely resemble our Proust, their Einstein may have produced an entirely new conception of the universe. But it is also possible that we will discover that the Papuans have virtually no literary tradition, just as many cultures have gone on for thousands of years without philosophy. Equally disconcerting, we may find out that the Papuans have only a very rudimentary understanding of the operations of the natural world. In this case we cannot reasonably continue to insist that Papuan culture is fully equal to Islamic and Hindu and Western culture. It is sheer intellectual dishonesty to proclaim, "The best we can say is that Papuan culture is simply *different* from other cultures." Rather, we must revise our relativist assumption and conclude, wistfully perhaps, that Papuan culture is in some respects inferior.

I emphasize the phrase "in some respects." I am not suggesting that there is any absolute standard by which one can proclaim cultures superior or inferior. The Papuans could excel in other areas, such as face painting or coconut juggling. There is no set of norms in the Platonic empyrean by which we can objectively rank cultures. Nor is there any purpose in staging a cultural Olympics that awards general prizes for "superiority" and "inferiority." Certainly groups and nations are free to dispute the criteria by which progress and excellence are usually judged. The Amish, for instance, reject many aspects of modernity. They generally avoid cars and telephones, although I recently read that they have established a website to market their products. Even so, the Amish clearly value the solidarity of their community over the convenience of many of our technological contrivances. They have chosen to go their own way. And nobody considers the Amish "inferior" for this.

But the situation is very different when one considers, for example, the main racial groups in America. Despite their various differences, Asian-Americans, blacks, Hispanics, and whites in the United States have the same objectives: all want to be in the entering class at Berkeley and Yale, all would like more seats in the boardroom at Microsoft and General Electric, all seek a greater representation in the Congress. When groups agree on the prize, when they define success in a similar way, it is entirely reasonable to ask which cultural strategy is the most effective to achieve this goal. As I have earlier argued, the assimilation strategy of the immigrants is simply superior in today's world to the protest strategy employed by African-American leaders, because it leads to more rapid upward mobility and economic success.

But the concept of cultural superiority need not be limited to groups contending for a specific prize. One might also find some cultures to be superior to others in achieving universal aspirations. Do such aspirations exist? Of course they do. Anthropologist Donald Brown provides a list of them in his book *Human Universals*.[4] One such universal aspiration is the desire to speak one's mind. In the West we call this the "right to free speech." But of course this "right" is not recognized in many cultures. In the late 1980s, the novelist Salman Rushdie made some satirical references to the prophet Muhammad in his book *The Satanic Verses*. The Islamic world was not convulsed with laughter, and in February 1989, the Ayatollah Khomeini issued a *fatwa* calling on Muslims to punish Rushdie for his crime of blasphemy by killing him.

Rushdie, heretofore known as an intrepid iconoclast and debunker of Western civilization, now begged the West to protect his life. Rushdie and a group of writers held a press conference in America in which they indignantly accused the Ayatollah Khomeini of not having sufficient regard for the First Amendment! Rushdie himself called the Ayatollah's attention to the works of John Stuart Mill.[5] Unfortunately Khomeini was not well schooled in the rhetoric of multiculturalism; otherwise he could have replied, "What gives you the right to impose your Western values on me? You have your cultural values, and I have my cultural values, and mine are just as valid as yours. Your values give priority to free speech, but my values give priority to outlawing blasphemy. Rushdie is free to express his cultural values by saying whatever he wants about Islam. And I am free to express my cultural values and order that his head be chopped off."

This is impeccable multicultural logic, and if the doctrine of cultural relativism holds true, then the Muslims would seem to be fully justified in attempting to murder Rushdie. The only way to make the case against such an action is to argue that the principle of free speech may be Western *in its origin* but it is universal *in its application*. This is another way of saying that the Declaration of Independence and the United Nations charter are correct: there are universal human rights. These rights may not always be recognized or upheld. But the failure of a government to enforce them at a given time does not invalidate the right. To recall Lincoln's statement that I cited earlier: the right has been declared so that the enforcement can follow when the circumstances allow.

By denying that there are universal standards of human rights, multiculturalists become de facto apologists for tyranny. They are so concerned about one culture "imposing its morality" on another that they ignore the fact that such impositions are sometimes indispensable to protect human dignity. Early in the nineteenth century the British outlawed the ancient Indian practice of *sati*. This custom called for widows to be tossed onto the burning pyres of their husbands.[6] The British also passed laws restricting child marriage, female infanticide, human sacrifice, and the caste system. In curbing these charming indigenous customs, the British were clearly imposing Western morality on their colonial subjects. But who today will dispute the results? Multicultural textbooks are strangely silent on these questions.

The doctrine that all people have certain basic rights does depend, I will concede, on a certain conception of human nature, one that ascribes a certain special quality or sacredness to humanity. There are other human aspirations, however, whose universality does not depend upon a philosophical premise of this sort. Recently I was visiting my family in Bombay, and I noticed that, on the outskirts of the city, a group of American anthropologists had set up camp to study the displaced peasants living in huts. As one scholar emerged from his tent, sporting his blue jeans and adjusting his zoom-lens camera, the peasants eyed him enviously. They eagerly told him, "We want your jeans! We want your camera!" Appalled at this suggestion, the anthropologist drew himself to full height and said, "But I am not here to convince you that our way of life is better. Oh no, I am merely here to study you. I believe that your culture is fully equal to ours. In fact, in some respect you are spared from the rat race, you are closer to nature, you are ecological saints." The peasants cogitated over these remarks and then repeated in unison, "We want your jeans! We want your camera!"

This example illustrates the point that in today's world there is a one-way movement from tribal, agrarian cultures toward modern, industrialized, American-style culture. Another way to put it is that people who go from wearing wooden shoes to wearing leather shoes will never go back to wearing wooden shoes. People identify America with triumph over necessity, with comfort, and with a longer life. Are there any societies that do not want these things? The very concept of "underdeveloped" nations, of nations seeking "development," shows that the poor countries of the world are unanimous about wanting to get richer. Until we can find cultures that prefer hunger rather than plenty, disease rather than health, and short lives rather than long ones, we have to acknowledge that material improvement is a universal objective.

Indeed, this is what Adam Smith said in his *Wealth of Nations:* "the desire of bettering our condition...comes with us from the womb and never leaves us till we go to the grave."[7] If this is true, then Francis Fukuyama is right that there is an inevitable progression from societies that thwart these human desires to societies that fulfill them. This isn't necessarily the "end of history," but it probably represents the end of primitive cultures. Moreover, given the things that people want, it is entirely reasonable to posit that some cultures (say, capitalist cultures with a Protestant heritage) are superior to other cultures (say, African socialist regimes or Islamic theocracies) in achieving these shared human objectives.

Cultural relativism collapses in the face of these universal aspirations. This was recognized by one of the Pied Pipers of relativism, the French anthropologist Claude Lévi-Strauss. For decades, Lévi-Strauss had emphatically insisted that so-called primitive cultures were just as complex and sophisticated as so-called advanced cultures. Lévi-Strauss labored ingeniously, in books like *The Savage Mind* and *Tristes Tropiques,* to show the equal value of these remote cultures. But then Lévi-Strauss made an alarming discovery: the people in those remote cultures don't want to stay in those cultures. If given the choice, they would prefer to live as Westerners do rather than as their ancestors did. Once he digested this disturbing fact, Lévi-Strauss gave up. In a stunning admission, he wrote, "The dogma of cultural relativism is challenged by the very people for whose moral benefit the anthropologists established it in the first place. The complaint the underdeveloped countries advance is not that they are being Westernized, but that there is too much delay in giving them the means to Westernize themselves. It is of no use to defend the individuality of human cultures against those cultures themselves."8

This is a devastating blow for the relativist ideology. Equally crushing are the actions of the immigrants, who are walking refutations of cultural relativism. When immigrants decide to leave their home country and move to another country, they are voting with their feet in favor of the new culture and against their native culture. Leaving one's country is a serious step. It involves giving up the community in which you have been raised, abandoning your family, severing your relationships with relatives and friends. You are imperiling your entire place in the world by going from a place where you are somebody to a place where you are nobody. People do not make such decisions whimsically. So why would immigrants voluntarily uproot themselves and relocate to another society unless they were deeply convinced that, on balance, the new culture was better than the old culture? Anyone who actually believed the multicultural nonsense that all cultures are equal would never leave home.

The triumph of American ideas and culture in the global marketplace, and the fact that most immigrants from around the world choose to come to the United States, would seem to be sufficient grounds for establishing the superiority of American civilization. But this is not entirely so, because we have not shown that the people of the world are *justified* in preferring the American way of life to any other. We must contend with the Islamic fundamentalists' argument that their societies are based on high principles while America is based on low principles. The Islamic critics are happy to concede the attractions of America, but they insist that these attractions are base. America, they say, appeals to what is most degraded about human nature; by contrast, Islamic societies may be poor and "backward," but they at least aspire to virtue. Even if they fall short, they are trying to live by God's law.

Americans usually have a hard time answering this argument, in part because they are bewildered by its theological cadences.

The usual tendency is to lapse into a kind of unwitting relativism. "You are following what you believe is right, and we are living by the values that we think are best." This pious buncombe usually concludes with a Rodney King–style plea for tolerance, "So why don't we learn to appreciate our differences? Why don't we just get along?" To see why this argument fails completely, imagine that you are living during the time of the Spanish Inquisition. The Grand Inquisitor is just starting to pull out your fingernails. You make the Rodney King move on him. "Torquemada, please stop pulling out my fingernails. Why don't we learn to appreciate our differences?" Most of us probably realize that Torquemada would not find this persuasive. But it is less obvious why he would not. Let me paraphrase Torquemada's argument: "You think I am taking away your freedom, but I am concerned with your immortal soul. Ultimately virtue is far more important than freedom. Our lives last for a mere second in the long expanse of eternity. What measure of pleasure or pain we experience in our short life is trivial compared to our fate in the never ending life to come. I am trying to save your soul from damnation. Who cares if you have to let out a few screams in the process? My actions are entirely for your own benefit. You should be *thanking me* for pulling out your fingernails."

I have recalled the Spanish Inquisition to make the point that the Islamic argument is one that we have heard before. We should not find it so strange that people think this way; it is the way that many in our own civilization used to think not so very long ago. The reason that most of us do not think this way now is that Western history has taught us a hard lesson. That lesson is that when the institutions of religion and government are one, and the secular authority is given the power to be the interpreter and enforcer of God's law, then horrible abuses of power are perpetrated in God's name. This is just what we saw in Afghanistan with the Taliban, and what we see now in places like Iran. This is not to suggest that Islam's historical abuses are worse than those of the West. But the West, as a consequence of its experience, learned to disentangle the institutions of religion and government—a separation that was most completely achieved in the United States. As we have seen, the West also devised a new way of organizing society around the institutions of science, democracy, and capitalism. The Renaissance, the Reformation, the Enlightenment, and the Scientific Revolution were some of the major signposts on Western civilization's road to modernity.

By contrast, the Islamic world did not have a Renaissance or a Reformation. No Enlightenment or Scientific Revolution either. Incredible though it may seem to many in the West, Islamic societies today are in some respects not very different from how they were a thousand years ago. Islam has been around for a long time. This brings us to a critical question: why are we seeing this upsurge of Islamic fundamentalism and Islamic fanaticism now?

To answer this question, we should recall that Islam was once one of the greatest and most powerful civilizations in the world. Indeed, there was a time when it seemed as if the whole world would fall under Islamic rule. Within a century of the prophet Muhammad's death, his converts had overthrown the Sassanid dynasty in Iran and conquered large tracts of territory from the Byzantine dynasty. Soon the Muslims had established an empire greater than that of Rome at its zenith. Over the next several centuries, Islam made deep inroads into Africa, Southeast Asia, and southern Europe. The crusades were launched to repel the forces of Islam, but the crusades ended in failure. By the sixteenth century, there were no fewer than five Islamic empires, unified by political ties, a common religion, and a common culture: the Mamluk sultans in Egypt, the Safavid dynasty in Iran, the Mughal empire in India, the empire of the Great Khans in Russia and Central Asia, and the Ottoman Empire based in Turkey. Of these, the Ottomans were by far the most formidable. They ruled most of North Africa, and threatened Mediterranean Europe and Austria. Europe was terrified that they might take over all the lands of Christendom. In all of history, Islam is the only non-Western civilization to pose a mortal threat to the West.

Then it all went wrong. Starting in the late seventeenth century, when the West was able to repel the Ottoman siege of Vienna, the power of Islam began a slow but steady decline. By the nineteenth century the Ottoman Empire was known as the "sick man of Europe," and it collapsed completely after World War I, when the victorious European powers carved it up and parceled out the pieces. Not only did the Muslims lose most of the territory they had conquered, but they also found themselves being ruled, either directly or indirectly, by the West. Today, even though colonialism has ended, the Islamic world is in a miserable state. Basically all that it has to offer is oil, and as technology opens up alternative sources of energy, even that will not amount to much. Without its oil revenues, the Islamic world will find itself in the position of sub-Saharan Africa: it will cease to matter. Even now it does not matter very much. The only reason it makes the news is by killing people. When is the last time you opened the newspaper to read about a great Islamic discovery or invention? While China and India, two other empires that were eclipsed by the West, have embraced Western technology and even assumed a leadership role in some areas, Islam's contribution to modern science and technology is negligible.

In addition to these embarrassments, the Islamic world faces a formidable threat from the United States. This is not the threat of American force or of American support for Israel. Israel is an irritant, but it does not threaten the existence of Islamic society. By contrast, America stands for an idea that is fully capable of transforming the Islamic world by winning the hearts of Muslims. The subversive American idea is one of shaping your own life, of making your own destiny, of following a path illumined not by external authorities but by your inner self. This American idea endangers the sanctity of the Muslim home, as well as the authority of Islamic society. It empowers women and children to assert their prerogatives against the male head of the household. It also undermines political and religious hierarchies. Of all American ideas, the "inner voice" is the most dangerous because it rivals the voice of Allah as a source of moral allegiance. So Islam is indeed, as bin Laden warned, facing the greatest threat to its survival since the days of Muhammad.

In recent decades, a great debate has broken out in the Muslim world to account for Islamic decline and to formulate a response to it. One response—let us call it the reformist or classical liberal response—is to acknowledge that the Islamic world has been left behind by modernity. The reformers' solution is to embrace science, democracy, and capitalism. This would mean adaptation—at least selective adaptation—to the ways of the West. The liberal reformers have an honorable intellectual tradition, associated with such names as Muhammad Abduh, Jamal al-Afghani, Muhammad Iqbal, and Taha Husayn. This group also enjoys a fairly strong base of support in the Muslim middle class. In the past two decades, however, the reformers have been losing the argument in the Islamic world to their rival group, the fundamentalists.

Here, in short, is the fundamentalist argument. The Koran promises that if Muslims are faithful to Allah, they will enjoy prosperity in this life and paradise in the next life. According to the fundamentalists, the Muslims were doing this for centuries, and they were invincible. But now, the fundamentalists point out, Islam is not winning any more; in fact, it is losing. What could be the reason for this? From the fundamentalist point of view, the answer is obvious: Muslims are not following the true teaching of Allah! The fundamentalists allege that Muslims have fallen away from the true faith and are mindlessly pursuing the ways of the infidel. The fundamentalists also charge that Islamic countries are now ruled by self-serving despots who serve as puppets for America and the West. The solution, the fundamentalists say, is to purge American troops and Western influence from the Middle East; to overthrow corrupt, pro-Western regimes like the ones in Pakistan, Egypt, and Saudi Arabia; and to return to the pure, original teachings of the Koran. Only then, the fundamentalists insist, can Islam recover its lost glory.

One can see, from this portrait, that the fundamentalists are a humiliated people who are seeking to recover ancestral greatness. They are not complete "losers": they are driven by an awareness of moral superiority, combined with political, economic, and military inferiority. Their argument has a powerful appeal to proud Muslims who find it hard to come to terms with their contemporary irrelevance. And so the desert wind of fundamentalism has spread throughout the Middle East. It has replaced Arab nationalism as the most powerful political force in the region.

The success of the fundamentalists in the Muslim world should not blind us from recognizing that their counterattack against America and the West is fundamentally defensive. The fundamentalists know that their civilization does not have the appeal to expand outside its precinct. It's not as if the Muslims were plotting to take, say, Australia. It is the West that is making incursions into Islamic territory, winning converts and threatening to subvert ancient loyalties and transform a very old way of life. So the fundamentalists are lashing out against this new, largely secular, Western "crusade." Terrorism, their weapon of counterinsurgency, is the weapon of the weak. Terrorism is the international equivalent of that domestic weapon of discontent: the riot. Political scientist Edward Banfield once observed that a riot is a failed revolution. People who know how to take over the government don't throw stones at a bus. Similarly terrorism of the bin Laden variety is a desperate strike against a civilization that the fundamentalists know they have no power to conquer.

But they do have the power to disrupt and terrify the people of America and the West. This is one of their goals, and their attack on September 11, 2001, was quite successful in this regard. But there is a second goal: to unify the Muslim world behind the fundamentalist banner and to foment uprisings against pro-Western regimes. Thus the bin Ladens of the world are waging a two-front war: against Western influence in the Middle East and against pro-Western governments and liberal influences within the Islamic world. So the West is not faced with a pure "clash of civilizations." It is not "the West" against "Islam." It is a clash of civilizations within the Muslim world. One side or the other will prevail.

So what should American policy be toward the region? It is a great mistake for Americans to believe that their country is hated because it is misunderstood. It is hated because it is understood only too well. Sometimes people say to me, "But the mullahs have a point about American culture. They are right about Jerry Springer." Yes, they are right about Springer. If we could get them to agree to stop bombing our facilities in return for us shipping them Jerry Springer to do with as they like, we should make the deal tomorrow, and throw in some of Springer's guests. But the Islamic fundamentalists don't just object to the excesses of American liberty: they object to liberty itself. Nor can we appease them by staying out of their world. We live in an age in which the flow of information is virtually unstoppable. We do not have the power to keep our ideals and our culture out of their lives.

Thus there is no alternative to facing their hostility. First, we need to destroy their terrorist training camps and networks. This is not easy to do, because some of these facilities are in countries like Iraq, Iran, Libya, and the Sudan. The U.S. should demand that those countries dismantle their terror networks and stop being incubators of terrorism. If they do not, we should work to get rid of their governments. How this is done is a matter of prudence. In some cases, such as Iraq, the direct use of force might be the answer. In others, such as Iran, the U.S. can capitalize on widespread popular dissatisfaction with the government.[9] Iran has a large middle class, with strong democratic and pro-American elements. But the dissenters are sorely in need of leadership, resources, and an effective strategy to defeat the ruling theocracy.

The U.S. also has to confront the fact that regimes allied with America, such as Pakistan, Egypt, and Saudi Arabia, are undemocratic, corrupt, and repressive. Indeed, the misdoings and tyranny of these regimes strengthen the cause of the fundamentalists, who are able to tap deep veins of popular discontent. How do the regimes deal with this fundamentalist resistance? They subsidize various religious and educational programs administered by the fundamentalists that teach terrorism and hatred of America. By focusing the people's discontent against a foreign target, the United States, the regimes of Saudi Arabia, Egypt, and Pakistan hope to divert attention from their own failings. The United States must make it clear to its Muslim allies that this "solution" is unacceptable. If they want American aid and American support, they must stop funding mosques and schools that promote terrorism and anti-Americanism. Moreover, they must take steps to reduce corruption, expand civil liberties, and enfranchise their people.

In the long term, America's goal is a large and difficult one: to turn Muslim fundamentalists into classical liberals. This does not mean that we want them to stop being Muslims. It does mean, however, that we want them to practice their religion *in the liberal way*. Go to a Promise Keepers meeting in Washington, D.C., or another of America's big cities. You will see tens of thousands of men singing, praying, hugging, and pledging chastity to their wives. A remarkable sight. These people are mostly evangelical and fundamentalist Christians. They are apt to approach you with the greeting, "Let me tell you what Jesus Christ has meant to my life." They want you to accept Christ, but their appeal is not to force but to consent. They do not say, "Accept Christ or I am going to plunge a dagger into your chest." Even the fundamentalist Christians in the West are liberals: they are practicing Christianity "in the liberal way."

The task of transforming Muslim fundamentalists into classical liberals will not be an easy one to perform in the Islamic world, where there is no tradition of separating religion and government. We need not require that Islamic countries adopt America's strict form of separation, which prohibits any government involvement in religion. But it is indispensable that Muslim fundamentalists relinquish the use of force for the purpose of spreading Islam. They, too, should appeal to consent. If this seems like a ridiculous thing to ask of Muslims, let us remember that millions of Muslims are already living this way. These are, of course, the Muslim immigrants to Europe and the United States. They are following the teachings of their faith, but most of them understand that they must respect the equal rights of others. They have renounced the *jihad* of the sword and confine themselves to the *jihad* of the pen and the *jihad* of the heart. In general, the immigrants are showing the way for Islam to change in the same way that Christianity changed in order to survive and flourish in the modern world.

Whether America can succeed in the mammoth enterprises of stopping terrorism and liberalizing the Islamic world depends a good deal on the people in the Middle East and a great deal on us. Fundamentalist Islam has now succeeded Soviet communism as the organizing theme of American foreign policy. Thus our newest challenge comes from a very old adversary. The West has been battling Islam for more than a thousand years. It is possible that this great battle has now been resumed, and that over time we will come to see the seventy-year battle against communism as a short detour.

But are we up to the challenge? There are some who think we are not. They believe that Americans are a divided people: not even a nation, but a collection of separate tribes. The multiculturalists actually proclaim this to be a good thing, and they strive to encourage people to affirm their differences. If, however, the multiculturalists are right in saying that "all we have in common is our diversity," then it follows that we have *nothing* in common. This does not bode well for the national unity that is a prerequisite to fighting against a determined foe. If the ethnic group is the primary unit of allegiance, why should we make sacrifices for people who come from ethnic groups other than our own? Doesn't a nation require a loyalty that transcends ethnic particularity?

Of course it does. And fortunately America does command such a loyalty. The multiculturalists are simply wrong about America, and despite their best efforts to promote a politics of difference, Americans remain a united people with shared values and a common way of life. There are numerous surveys of national attitudes that confirm this,[10] but it is most easily seen when Americans are abroad. Hang out at a Parisian café, for instance, and you can easily pick out the Americans: they dress the same way, eat the same food, listen to the same music, and laugh at the same jokes. However different their personalities, Americans who run into each other in remote places always become fast friends. And even the most jaded Americans who spend time in other countries typically return home with an intense feeling of relief and a new-found appreciation for the routine satisfactions of American life.

It is easy to forget the cohesiveness of a free people in times of peace and prosperity. New York is an extreme example of the great pandemonium that results when countless individuals and groups pursue their diverse interests in the normal course of life. In a crisis, however, the national tribe comes together, and this is exactly what happened in New York and the rest of America following the terrorist attack. Suddenly political, regional, and racial differences evaporated; suddenly Americans stood as one. This surprised many people, including many Americans, who did not realize that, despite the centrifugal forces that pull us in different directions, there is a deep national unity that holds us together.

Unity, however, is not sufficient for the challenges ahead. America also needs the moral self-confidence to meet its adversary. This is the true lesson of Vietnam: Americans cannot succeed unless they are convinced that they are fighting on behalf of the good. There are some, as we have seen, who fear that America no longer stands for what is good. They allege that American freedom produces a licentious, degenerate society that is scarcely worth defending. We return, therefore, to the question of what America is all about, and whether this country, in its dedication to the principle of freedom, subverts the higher principle of virtue.

The central themes of American life can be seen in F. Scott Fitzgerald's novel *The Great Gatsby.* The protagonist is typically American in that he has invented his own identity: James Gatz has become Jay Gatsby. On the surface, Gatsby is a great American success story, yet Fitzgerald also portrays a darker side—

Gatsby fabricates his credentials, he hangs out with shady figures, and his wealth has probably been acquired illegally. Moreover, Gatsby is a man of questionable judgment: he loves a woman, Daisy, who is vain and callous. He foolishly thinks that his great wealth can buy her affections and somehow erase the past. These are typical American illusions, and Gatsby pays a high price for them—he ends up dead in the swimming pool.

Even so, Gatsby is Fitzgerald's hero—he is truly the "great" Gatsby—because he represents the magical self-transformation of the individual in a new kind of society. And in Fitzgerald's view he is redeemed by the magnitude of his aspirations. There is "something gorgeous about him," "some heightened sensitivity to the promises of life," and an "extraordinary gift for hope." Gatsby's life is a reminder of the astonishment and wonder with which the first Dutch sailors beheld the new world, a world that signals the fulfillment of "the last and greatest of all human dreams."[11] Fitzgerald's conclusion is that America still holds out that kind of promise. He implies, and I agree with him, that there is something unexpected, turbocharged, and exhilarating about living in such a society. It is simply more fun than living elsewhere.

So what about virtue? The fundamental difference between the society that the Islamic fundamentalists want and the society that Americans have is that the Islamic activists seek a country where the life of the citizens is *directed by others,* while Americans live in a nation where the life of the citizens is largely *self-directed.* The central goal of American freedom is self-reliance: the individual is placed in the driver's seat of his own life. The Islamic fundamentalists presume the moral superiority of the externally directed life on the grounds that it is aimed at virtue.

The self-directed life, however, also seeks virtue—virtue realized not through external command but, as it were, "from within." The real question is: which type of society is more successful in achieving the goal of virtue?

Let us concede at the outset that, in a free society, freedom will frequently be used badly. Freedom, by definition, includes freedom to do good or evil, to act nobly or basely. Thus we should not be surprised that there is a considerable amount of vice, licentiousness, and vulgarity in a free society. Given the warped timber of humanity, freedom is simply an expression of human flaws and weaknesses. But if freedom brings out the worst in people, it also brings out the best. The millions of Americans who live decent, praiseworthy lives deserve our highest admiration because they have opted for the good when the good is not the only available option. Even amidst the temptations that a rich and free society offers, they have remained on the straight path. Their virtue has special luster because it is freely chosen. The free society does not guarantee virtue any more than it guarantees happiness. But it allows for the pursuit of both, a pursuit rendered all the more meaningful and profound because success is not guaranteed: it has to be won through personal striving.

By contrast, the externally directed life that Islamic fundamentalists seek undermines the possibility of virtue. If the supply of virtue is insufficient in self-directed societies, it is almost nonexistent in externally directed societies because coerced virtues are not virtues at all. Consider the woman who is required to wear a veil. There is no modesty in this, because the woman is being compelled. Compulsion cannot produce virtue: it can only produce the outward semblance of virtue. And once the reins of coercion are released, as they were for the terrorists who lived in the United States, the worst impulses of human nature break loose. Sure enough, the deeply religious terrorists spent their last days in gambling dens, bars, and strip clubs, sampling the licentious lifestyle they were about to strike out against.[12] In this respect they were like the Spartans, who—Plutarch tells us—were abstemious in public but privately coveted wealth and luxury. In externally directed societies, the absence of freedom signals the absence of virtue. Thus the free society is not simply richer, more varied, and more fun: it is also morally superior to the externally directed society. There is no reason for anyone, least of all the cultural conservatives, to feel hesitant about rising to the defense of our free society.

Even if Americans possess the necessary unity and self-confidence, there is also the question of nerve. Some people, at home and abroad, are skeptical that America can endure a long war against Islamic fundamentalism because they consider Americans to be, well, a little bit soft. As one of bin Laden's lieutenants put it, "Americans love life, and we love death." His implication was that Americans do not have the stomach for the kind of deadly, drawn-out battle that the militant Muslims are ready to fight. This was also the attitude of the Taliban. "Come and get us," they taunted America. "We are ready for *jihad*. Come on, you bunch of weenies." And then the Taliban was hit by a juggernaut of American firepower that caused their regime to disintegrate within a couple of weeks. Soon the Taliban leadership had headed for the caves, or for Pakistan, leaving their captured soldiers to beg for their lives. Even the call of *jihad* and the promise of martyrdom could not stop these hard men from—in the words of Mullah Omar himself—"running like chickens with their heads cut off." This is not to say that Americans should expect all its battles against terrorism and Islamic fundamentalism to be so short and so conclusive. But neither should America's enemies expect Americans to show any less firmness or fierceness than they themselves possess.

Although much of America is immersed in Rousseau's ethic of authenticity, there are sizable segments of the culture that have not been infiltrated by it. The firefighters and policemen who raced into the burning towers of the World Trade Center showed that their lives were dedicated to something higher than "self-fulfillment." The same can be said of Todd Beamer and his fellow passengers who forced the terrorists to crash United Airlines Flight 93 in the woods of western Pennsylvania rather than flying on to Camp David or the White House. Authenticity, thank God, is not the operating principle of the U.S. military. America's enemies should not expect to do battle against the Starbucks guy. The military has its own culture, which is closer to that of the firefighters and policemen, and also bears an affinity with the culture of the "greatest generation." Only now are those Americans who grew up during the 1960s coming to appreciate the virtues—indeed the indispensability—of this older, sturdier culture of courage, nobility, and sacrifice. It is this culture that will protect the liberties of all Americans, including that of the Starbucks guy.

As the American founders knew, America is a new kind of society that produces a new kind of human being. That human being—confident, self-reliant, tolerant, generous, future oriented—is a vast improvement over the wretched, servile, fatalistic, and intolerant human being that traditional societies have always produced, and that Islamic societies produce now. In America, the life we are given is not as important as the life we make. Ultimately, America is worthy of our love and sacrifice because, more than any other society, it makes possible the good life, and the life that is good.

America is the greatest, freest, and most decent society in existence. It is an oasis of goodness in a desert of cynicism and barbarism. This country, once an experiment unique in the world, is now the last best hope for the world. By making sacrifices for America, and by our willingness to die for her, we bind ourselves by invisible cords to those great patriots who fought at Yorktown, Gettysburg, and Iwo Jima, and we prove ourselves worthy of the blessings of freedom. By defeating the terrorist threat posed by Islamic fundamentalism, we can protect the American way of life while once again redeeming humanity from a global menace. History will view America as a great gift to the world, a gift that Americans today must preserve and cherish.

NOTES

PREFACE

1. Thucydides, *History of the Peloponnesian War* (New York: Penguin Books, 1986), 144–51.

CHAPTER ONE

1. "Notes Found After the Hijackings," *New York Times*, 29 September 2001, B-3.
2. John O'Sullivan, "Volatile Ideas That Bombs Can't Destroy," *San Diego Union-Tribune*, 14 October 2001, G-1.
3. Nada El Sawy, "Yes, I Follow Islam, but I'm Not a Terrorist," *Newsweek*, 15 October 2001, 12.

4. Hendrik Hertzberg and David Remnick, "The Trap," *New Yorker,* 1 October 2001, 38.

5. Joseph Lelyveld, "The Mind of a Suicide Bomber," *New York Times Magazine,* 28 October 2001, 50.

6. "Don't Count on Muslim Support," *The American Enterprise,* December 2001, 11.

7. I understand the limitations of the term "fundamentalism," which refers to a specifically American Protestant movement to return to biblical fundamentals. I use the term here to refer to Muslims who are seeking to return the Islamic world to a purer version of Islam unadulterated by non-Islamic ideas and influences.

8. *The Koran,* trans. N. J. Dawood (New York: Penguin Books, 1995), 186.

9. Ibn Khaldun, *The Muqaddimah* (Princeton: Princeton University Press, 1967), 183.

10. Bernard Lewis, *The Muslim Discovery of Europe* (New York: W. W. Norton, 1982), 60–61; see also Bernard Lewis, "Jihad vs. Crusade," *Wall Street Journal,* 27 September 2001.

11. For readings on the meaning of *jihad,* see Rudolph Peters, *Jihad in Classical and Modern Islam* (Princeton: Markus Wiener Publishers, 1996).

12. Francis Fukuyama, *The End of History and the Last Man* (New York: Avon Books, 1992).

13. Samuel Huntington, *The Clash of Civilizations and the Remaking of World Order* (New York: Touchstone Books, 1997), 20.

14. Lee Kuan Yew, "America Is No Longer Asia's Model," *New Perspectives Quarterly,* Winter 1996; Fareed Zakaria, "A Conversation with Lee Kuan Yew," *Foreign Affairs,* March–April 1994.

15. John Esposito, ed., "Sayyid Qutb: Ideologue of Islamic Revival," in *Voices of Resurgent Islam* (New York: Oxford University Press, 1983); John Esposito, *The Islamic Threat: Myth or Reality?* (New York: Oxford University Press, 1999), 135–37; Ibrahim Abu-Rabi, *Intellectual Origins of Islamic*

Resurgence in the Modern Arab World (Albany: State University of New York Press, 1996), 133, 158, 172; Roxanne Euben, "Pre-modern, Anti-modern or Postmodern: Islamic and Western Critiques of Modernity," *Review of Politics,* Summer 1997, 434–50.

16. "The End of Democracy?" *First Things,* November 1996, 18–42.

17. Patrick J. Buchanan, *The Death of the West* (New York: St. Martin's Press, 2001), 6.

18. Cited in "Idiocy Watch," *New Republic,* 15 October 2001, 10.

19. Ann Gerhart, "Black Caucus Waves the Caution Flag," *Washington Post,* 28 September 2001, C-1, C-8.

20. James Bowman, "Towers of Intellect," *Wall Street Journal,* 5 October 2001.

21. Stanley Kurtz, "Edward Said, Imperialist," *Weekly Standard,* 8 October 2001, 35.

22. These words, from the writer Arundhati Roy, were quoted in "Sontagged," *Weekly Standard,* 15 October 2001, 42–43.

23. Cornel West, *Keeping Faith: Philosophy and Race in America* (New York: Routledge, 1993), 236.

24. Ali Mazrui, "Islamic and Western Values," *Foreign Affairs,* September–October 1997.

25. Nathan Irvin Huggins, *Black Odyssey: The African-American Ordeal in Slavery* (New York: Vintage Books, 1990), 113.

26. Dennis Farney, "As America Triumphs, Americans Are Awash in Doubt," *Wall Street Journal,* 27 July 1992, A-1; see also John Hope Franklin, "The Moral Legacy of the Founding Fathers," *University of Chicago Magazine,* Summer 1975, 10–13.

27. Stanley Fish, *There's No Such Thing as Free Speech, and It's a Good Thing Too* (New York: Oxford University Press, 1994), 87.

28. Haki Madhubuti, *Black Men: Obsolete, Single, Dangerous?* (Chicago: Third World Press, 1990), 28.

29. Edmund Burke, *Reflections on the Revolution in France* (New York: Penguin Books, 1982), 172.

30. Martha Nussbaum, "Genesis of a Book," *Liberal Education,* Spring 1999, 38.
31. Alexis de Tocqueville, *Democracy in America* (New York: Vintage Books, 1990), Vol. I, 394, Vol. II, 22.

CHAPTER TWO

1. Kwame Anthony Appiah and Henry Louis Gates Jr., "Africa Can Regain Its Glory," *Wall Street Journal,* 28 January 2000; Steve Hanke, "Africa and Economics," *Forbes,* 28 May 2001, 96.
2. Edward Said, *Orientalism* (New York: Vintage Books, 1978), 31; Edward Said, *Culture and Imperialism* (New York: Alfred A. Knopf, 1993), 8.
3. Jacques Gernet, *A History of Chinese Civilization* (Cambridge: Cambridge University Press, 1989); John Merson, *The Genius That Was China* (Woodstock, NY: The Overlook Press, 1990).
4. David Landes, *The Wealth and Poverty of Nations* (New York: W. W. Norton, 1998), 54.
5. Lewis, *The Muslim Discovery of Europe,* 68, 222; Bernard Lewis, *Islam and the West* (New York: Oxford University Press, 1993), 14.
6. Jared Diamond, *Guns, Germs, and Steel* (New York: W. W. Norton, 1997).
7. Walter Rodney, *How Europe Underdeveloped Africa* (Washington, D.C.: Howard University Press, 1982), 27.
8. Chinweizu, *The West and the Rest of Us* (New York: Vintage Books, 1975), 3.
9. Frantz Fanon, *The Wretched of the Earth* (New York: Grove Press, 1968), 76.
10. Steve Miller, "Black Leaders Set to Herald Causes," *Washington Times,* 29 November 2001.
11. Khaldun, *The Muqaddimah,* 375.

12. Louise Levathes, *When China Ruled the Seas* (New York: Oxford University Press, 1994); Philip Snow, *The Star Raft: China's Encounter with Africa* (Ithaca, NY: Cornell University Press, 1988).

13. Daniel Boorstin, *The Discoverers* (New York: Vintage Books, 1983), 199.

14. Orlando Patterson, *Slavery and Social Death: A Comparative Study* (Cambridge: Harvard University Press, 1982), vii.

15. J. M. Roberts, *The Penguin History of the World* (New York: Penguin Books, 1990), 727.

16. Roy Basler, ed., *The Collected Works of Abraham Lincoln* (New Brunswick, NJ: Rutgers University Press, 1953), Vol. II, 532.

17. The documentation for this is provided in my earlier work, *The End of Racism* (New York: Free Press, 1995), 105–6 and accompanying endnotes.

18. Henry Louis Gates, ed., *Bearing Witness* (New York: Pantheon Books, 1991), 35.

19. Peter Bauer, *Equality, the Third World, and Economic Delusion* (Cambridge: Harvard University Press, 1981), 67–68; Peter Bauer, *Reality and Rhetoric: Studies in the Economies of Development* (Cambridge: Harvard University Press, 1984), 2, 24.

20. Even the Christian notion of miracles does not invalidate the reasonableness of reality. Miracles represent rare acts of divine intervention. A miracle is something that contravenes the laws of nature. Thus the notion of miracles does not reject—indeed it depends on—the presumption that nature follows regular laws. The wonder that attends a miracle arises from the astonishment that these laws might be suspended through divine action.

21. Robert Nisbet, *The Making of Modern Society* (New York: New York University Press, 1986), 42.

22. J. B. Bury, *The Idea of Progress* (New York: Dover Publications, 1960), 111.

CHAPTER THREE

1. James Burnham, *Suicide of the West* (Washington, D.C.: Regnery Gateway, 1985), 15–18, 20, 24.

2. Jean Paul Sartre, introduction to Frantz Fanon, *The Wretched of the Earth* (New York: Grove Weidenfeld, 1963), 13, 27.

3. Mike Zwerin, "Birthday of the Cool," *Forbes,* 15 November 1999, 322.

4. Benjamin Barber, *Jihad vs. McWorld* (New York: Ballantine Books, 1996), 293.

5. Douglas Jehl, "It's Barbie vs. Laila and Sara in Mideast Culture War," *New York Times,* 2 June 1999, A-4.

6. Elaine Sciolino, "Who Hates the U.S.? Who Loves It?" *New York Times,* 23 September 2001.

7. Werner Sombart, *Why Is There No Socialism in the United States?* (White Plains: International Arts and Sciences Press, 1976), 109–10.

8. V. S. Naipaul, "Our Universal Civilization," *New York Review of Books,* 31 January 1991, 25.

9. Albert Hourani, *A History of the Arab Peoples* (Cambridge: Harvard University Press, 1991), 47; Lewis, *The Muslim Discovery of Europe,* 63.

10. Cited by Paul Rahe, *Republics, Ancient and Modern* (Charlotte: University of North Carolina Press, 1994), Vol. III, 53.

11. Madison, Hamilton, and Jay, *The Federalist Papers,* No. 10, Isaac Kramnick, ed. (London: Penguin Books, 1987), 124.

12. James Boswell, *The Life of Johnson* (New York: Oxford University Press, 1933), Vol. I, 567.

13. William Shakespeare, *Julius Caesar,* act 3, scene 2, lines 84–86.

14. Confucius, *The Analects* (New York: Penguin Books, 1986), 74.

15. Khaldun, *The Muqaddimah,* 313.

16. Madison, Hamilton, and Jay, *The Federalist Papers,* No. 51, 321.

17. Ibid., 320.

18. Romans 7:19, Revised Standard Version.

19. See, for example, Will Kymlicka, *Multicultural Citizens* (Oxford: Clarendon Press, 1995).

20. Cited by Michael Novak, *The Rise of the Unmeltable Ethnics* (New York: Macmillan, 1971), 140.

21. Cited by Reed Ueda, *Postwar Immigrant America* (Boston: St. Martin's Press, 1994), 124.

CHAPTER FOUR

1. Michael Barone, *The New Americans* (Washington, D.C.: Regnery Publishing, 2001), 19.

2. Thomas Jefferson, *Notes on the State of Virginia* (New York: W. W. Norton, 1982), 62–63, 138–40.

3. David Brion Davis, *The Problem of Slavery in Western Culture* (New York: Oxford University Press, 1988), 168.

4. Ralph Lerner, *The Thinking Revolutionary* (Ithaca: Cornell University Press, 1987), 163.

5. William McNeill, *Plagues and Peoples* (New York: Doubleday, 1976).

6. W. E. B. DuBois, *The Souls of Black Folk* (New York: W. W. Norton, 1999), 11.

7. Philip S. Foner, ed., *The Life and Writings of Frederick Douglass* (New York: International Publishers, 1950), Vol. I, 126, Vol. II, 188–89.

8. Franklin, "The Moral Legacy of the Founding Fathers," 10–13.

9. *Dred Scott v. Sandford*, 60 U.S. 393 (1857).

10. Frederick Douglass, "The American Constitution and the Slave: An Address Delivered in Glasgow, Scotland, on 26 March 1860," in John Blassingame, ed., *The Frederick Douglass Papers* (New Haven: Yale University Press, 1979–92), Vol. 3, 352.

11. Thomas Jefferson, letter to Henri Gregoire, February 25, 1809, in Merrill D. Peterson, ed., *The Portable Thomas Jefferson* (New York: Penguin Books, 1975), 517.

12. Jefferson, *Notes on the State of Virginia,* 163.

13. Davis, *The Problem of Slavery in Western Culture.*

14. Cited by Harry Jaffa, *Crisis of the House Divided* (Chicago: University of Chicago Press, 1959), 32.

15. Cited by Forrest McDonald, *Novus Ordo Seclorum* (Lawrence: University Press of Kansas, 1985), 160.

16. Jaffa, *Crisis of the House Divided,* 370.

17. Abraham Lincoln, "Speech on the Dred Scott Decision," 26 June 1857, in Mario Cuomo and Harold Holzer, eds., *Lincoln on Democracy* (New York: HarperCollins, 1990), 90–91.

18. Frederick Douglass, "Address for the Promotion of Colored Enlistments," 6 July 1863, in Foner, ed., *The Life and Writings of Frederick Douglass,* Vol. III, 365.

19. Cited by Herbert Storing, *Toward a More Perfect Union* (Washington, D.C.: AEI Press, 1995), 156.

20. Toni Morrison, *Playing in the Dark* (Cambridge: Harvard University Press, 1982), 20.

21. Derrick Bell, *Faces at the Bottom of the Well* (New York: Basic Books, 1992), 1, 3, 10, 152.

22. Richard Herrnstein and Charles Murray, *The Bell Curve* (New York: Free Press, 1994).

23. Wayne Camara and Amy Schmidt, "Group Differences in Standardized Testing and Social Stratification" (New York: College Entrance Examination Board, 1999), 17–18.

24. Laurence Steinberg, Sanford Dornbusch, and Bradford Brown, "Ethnic Differences in Adolescent Achievement," *American Psychologist,* June 1992, 723.

25. W. E. B. DuBois, *The Negro American Family* (Cambridge: MIT Press, 1970), first published in 1908.

26. Herbert Gutman, *The Black Family in Slavery and Freedom* (New York: Pantheon Books, 1976).

27. Daniel Patrick Moynihan, "The Negro Family: The Case for National Action," in Lee Rainwater and William Yancy, eds.,

The Moynihan Report and the Politics of Controversy (Cambridge: MIT Press, 1967).

28. William Julius Wilson, *The Truly Disadvantaged* (Chicago: University of Chicago Press, 1987).
29. Philip Kasinitz, *Caribbean New York* (Ithaca: Cornell University Press, 1992).

CHAPTER FIVE

1. Cited by Lewis, *The Muslim Discovery of Europe*, 286–87.
2. Cited by Gertrude Himmelfarb, *One Nation, Two Cultures* (New York: Alfred A. Knopf, 1999), 94.
3. Ronald Berman, ed., *Solzhenitsyn at Harvard* (Washington, D.C.: Ethics and Public Policy Center, 1980), 17.
4. Cited by J. Bottum, "AWOL Christian Soldiers?" *Weekly Standard*, 1 October 2001, 12.
5. Robert Bork, *Slouching Towards Gomorrah* (New York: Regan Books, 1996).
6. Seymour Martin Lipset, *American Exceptionalism* (New York: W. W. Norton, 1996), 61–62.
7. William Bennett, *The Index of Leading Cultural Indicators* (New York: Broadway, 1999).
8. Joseph Schumpeter, *Capitalism, Socialism, and Democracy* (New York: HarperPerennial, 1976), 84.
9. "Face of the Nation," *U.S. News & World Report*, 15 April 1996, 18.
10. Alan Ritter and Julia Bondanella, eds., *Rousseau's Political Writings* (New York: W. W. Norton, 1988), 192.
11. Jean-Jacques Rousseau, *Emile* (New York: Basic Books, 1979), 255.
12. Charles Taylor, *The Ethics of Authenticity* (Cambridge: Harvard University Press, 1991), 29.

13. Cited by Roger Masters, *The Political Philosophy of Rousseau* (Princeton: Princeton University Press, 1968), 212.

14. Jean-Jacques Rousseau, "Discourse on the Sciences and Arts," in Roger Masters, ed., *The First and Second Discourses* (New York: St. Martin's Press, 1964), 64.

15. Rousseau, *Emile,* 286.

16. Rousseau, "Discourse on the Sciences and Arts," 51.

17. Taylor, *The Ethics of Authenticity,* 27.

18. Jean-Jacques Rousseau, *Confessions* (New York: Alfred A. Knopf, 1992), 1.

19. Irving Babbit, *Rousseau and Romanticism* (New Brunswick, NJ: Transaction Books, 1991), 127.

20. St. Augustine, *Confessions* (New York: Penguin Books, 1961), 146.

21. "Transcendence," the philosopher Leo Strauss reminds us, "is not a preserve of revealed religion." See Leo Strauss, "Natural Right and the Historical Approach," in Hilail Gildin, ed., *An Introduction to Political Philosophy* (Detroit: Wayne State University Press, 1989), 105.

22. Charles Taylor, *Sources of the Self* (Cambridge: Harvard University Press, 1996), 16, 18, 27.

23. Clifford Orwin and Nathan Tarcov, eds., "Introduction," in *The Legacy of Rousseau* (Chicago: University of Chicago Press, 1997), xi.

24. Arthur Melzer, "Rousseau and the Modern Cult of Sincerity," in ibid, 277.

25. *Planned Parenthood v. Casey,* 505 U.S. 833 (1992).

26. Babbit, *Rousseau and Romanticism,* 5, 60, 63, 68, 128, 155.

27. Bork, *Slouching Towards Gomorrah,* 140–53.

28. Buchanan, *The Death of the West,* 262.

CHAPTER SIX

1. Thucydides, *History of the Peloponnesian War,* 401–5.

2. Henry Kissinger, *White House Years* (Boston: Little, Brown and Co., 1979), 54–70.

3. Joe Loconte, "Rumsfeld's Just War," *Weekly Standard,* 24 December 2001.

4. Donald Brown, *Human Universals* (Philadelphia: Temple University Press, 1991).

5. Salman Rushdie, "One Thousand Days in a Balloon," in Steve MacDonogh, ed., *The Rushdie Letters* (Lincoln: University of Nebraska Press, 1993), 122.

6. Sakuntala Narasimhan, *Sati: Widow Burning in India* (New York: Anchor Books, 1990).

7. Adam Smith, *The Wealth of Nations* (Chicago: University of Chicago Press, 1976), Vol. I, 362–63.

8. Claude Lévi-Strauss, "Race and History," in Leo Kuper, ed., *Race, Science, and Society* (Paris: UNESCO Press, 1975), 116.

9. See, for example, Amy Waldman, "In Iran, an Angry Generation Longs for Jobs, More Freedom, and Power," *New York Times,* 7 December 2001.

10. See, for example, John Fetto and Rebecca Gardyn, "An All-American Melting Pot," *American Demographics,* July 2001, 8. The survey was conducted by Maritz Marketing Research.

11. F. Scott Fitzgerald, *The Great Gatsby* (New York: Scribner, 1995), 6, 189.

12. Diane McWhorter, "Terrorists Tasted Lusty Lifestyle They So Despised," *USA Today,* 26 September 2001, 11-A.

ACKNOWLEDGMENTS

Although I began research for this book several years ago, it discusses themes that have engaged me since the time I came to the United States as an exchange student from Bombay, India, in 1978. Thus I cannot even begin to enumerate all the people who have contributed to this book. But I do want to single out my wife, Dixie, with whom I discuss these issues all the time; Michael Vetti, my diligent and uncomplaining research assistant; and Bruce Schooley, my most avid and helpful reader. I am grateful to the American Enterprise Institute and to its president, Christopher DeMuth, for the happy and productive decade I spent there. I also wish to thank my new employer, the Hoover Institution, and its president, John Raisian, for providing me with a base of operations and the freedom to read, think, and write. I am now the Rishwain Fellow at Hoover and appreciate the generosity of Robert and Karen Rishwain in supporting my current work. My thanks also go to the John M. Olin Foundation and its executive director, Jim Piereson, for vital support over the years. My agent, Rafe Sagalyn, was there for me, as always, and I have enjoyed working with my new editor at Regnery, Harry Crocker, who also happens to be an old friend. I also wish to acknowledge the advice and assistance of Sally Von Behren, T. Kenneth Cribb and the staff at the Intercollegiate Studies Institute, Philip Merrill, Doug and Pat Perry, Jason Pontin and the staff at *Red Herring*, Elizabeth Pungello and the W. H. Brady Foundation, Ron Robinson and the staff at the Young America's Foundation, Richard Schatz, Kenneth Simon, Mark Skousen and the staff at the Foundation for Economic Education, and Steven Wardell.

INDEX